WHO WAS THE LADY IN THE COFFIN

Charleston, SC
www.PalmettoPublishing.com

Paperback ISBN: 979-8-8229-4477-0

WHO WAS THE LADY IN THE COFFIN

Early History of Helena

STEVE PETKOFF

ACKNOWLEDGMENTS

This book required a laborious amount of research. I want to thank all those who assisted me in searching for the lady in the coffin. I spoke with numerous individuals over an extended period to see if they recalled any memories of this event. Those individuals are named herein at different intervals where applicable.

Angie Romine, the Lady's most recent family member, furnished valuable pictures, dates, and much other information for my search.

Others helped with my editing and proofreading—thanks to my sister Betty Hightower, her friend Cecilia Pontius, and my friend Becky Newberry.

Bobby Roberts, my second-grade schoolmate in Helena whom I later caught up with in college, provided his experience as a trained historian and insights about growing up in the area. He even wrote the foreword, which I am incredibly appreciative of.

Many others added several bits of information they recalled on Facebook.

Patty Smith advised me how and where to search for historical information and documents. She also let me use some of her published articles and gave me access to the Tri-County Genealogical Society, allowing me to look through records.

My wife, Pat, kept me on track with her expert computer skills each time I hit a technical glitch. She put up with my many complaints and shared my joyous moments.

I will forever be grateful to all these wonderful and generous friends for their encouragement and excitement.

TABLE OF CONTENTS

Foreword · · · · · viii

Chapter 1 "That Awful Thing" · · · · · 1
Chapter 2 Lingering Memories of a Coffin · · · · · 5
Chapter 3 Baby Formula Fund-Raiser · · · · · 16
Chapter 4 Learning the Landscape · · · · · 23
Chapter 5 Playground, Battleground, or Burial Ground? · · · · · 32
Chapter 6 A New City · · · · · 39
Chapter 7 Who Was She? · · · · · 48
Chapter 8 Water, Water, Everywhere—Number, Please · · · · · 57
Chapter 9 Get Out of the Mud · · · · · 66
Chapter 10 The Forgotten General · · · · · 73
Chapter 11 Hattie on the Hill · · · · · 87
Chapter 12 Secrets of the *Sultana* · · · · · *94*
Chapter 13 *The Curse of Oak Island* · · · · · 104
Chapter 14 Connecting the Dots · · · · · 110
Chapter 15 Unfalsifiable · · · · · 126
Chapter 16 Foolproof · · · · · 133

FOREWORD

In his earlier book, *Holly Street,* Steve Petkoff introduced us to his experiences growing up in Helena, Arkansas, in the 1940s and 1950s. Now, with his new book, *Who Was the Lady in the Coffin,* he has taken up the challenge of unraveling one of those great mysteries of his childhood.

Steve and I were both lucky enough to live in a small city that had not yet begun the relentless economic decline that has ravaged so much of the Mississippi River Delta. For white children, at least, it was a golden age. Our responsibilities were light, and we were free to roam the streets and hills looking for adventure. One of the many places that sung to our adventurous spirit was a high point on Cowley's Ridge, which circles part of old Helena. It was known as Reservoir Hill, and on a clear day and with luck, you might see the superstructure of a tow boat about two miles away on the Mississippi River. It was a fine place to spend some time.

However, in the old days, when Helena was a thriving antebellum river town, that same area was known as Graveyard Hill. And it was on that big pile of dirt that the winds pushed up eons ago that many of Helena's earliest citizens were buried. The reasons that spot was chosen seem obvious—it was high enough to avoid the floods that periodically inundated Helena, and it provided a fine view of the town.

Sometime after the Civil War Helena needed a high place for a reservoir, which was part of the city's plans to build a modern water system for the growing community. Graveyard Hill fit the bill nicely, but first, hundreds of graves had to be moved to another location. No doubt the locals did the best they could to locate and remove all the remains, but few burial records existed, and the area had been badly disrupted during the civil war. The reservoir was duly constructed, but it was not long before old coffins and remains began to appear, as rain and soil removal relentlessly disturbed the dirt that comprised most of Crowley's Ridge.

One day in the mid-nineteen fifties, when Steve and a couple of his buddies were exploring what was now Reservoir Hill, they came upon a most remarkable sight - a coffin with a broken glass face plate. Inside was the body of a grown female. It was, as Steve writes, his first view of someone in a coffin, and for him, it remained "an unforgettable memory." Time proved that what he saw that day was unforgettable, and, after more than six decades, Steve decided to try to solve the mystery of exactly who was in that coffin.

Steve had set for himself a formidable task because both the archeological and historical records on Graveyard Hill are practically nonexistent. Undeterred, he began his quest for information; along the way, he learned about many things - the explosions aboard *General Brown* and later the *Sultana,* the origins of the Cynthia Milk Fund, the founding of Helena, the development of the all-important water works there, and the scourge of Yellow Fever - to name only a few of the stories he discovered alongside his search for that elusive lady in the coffin. Those stories are related in this book and reflect his journey of historical self-discovery that reveals some of the colorful, odd, and important events that he studied while searching for the lady in the coffin. Those stories alone make reading the book worthwhile.

However, Steve never gave up on his original mission, and after a prodigious amount of research, he began to piece together a plausible theory of who that person might have been in the coffin he saw so many years ago.

A historian whose name I have long forgotten once remarked that no matter how hard we try you could never get to the "nub of history." By that he meant that the final truth will always be obscured because of such factors as the lack of documents, varying interpretations of those materials that have survived, and other limitations that time and space impose on the writer. All the historian can do is make the best use of the evidence that exists. Steve has done an admirable job running down even the most obscure sources, and he used them well. I leave it to the reader to decide how close he gets to that elusive nub.

Bobby Roberts

Chapter One

"THAT AWFUL THING"

"That awful thing," she said. She was the mother of my friend Dickey. Dickey was my age and lived at the corner of Poplar and York Streets in Helena with his mother, older sister, her husband, and their daughter. I genuinely liked his mother and sister. They were down-to-earth, very nice people. I always joked with his sister. His mother treated me like her own and periodically treated me like an adult by how we conversed. The daughter was quite a bit younger than us, so I don't remember much other than sometimes teasing her.

I've struggled to remember my exact age at this time, but I know I must have been very young. My best guess is that I was between 10 and 15. I was born in 1943, which equates to 1953 to 1958. A lot was going on in my life then. I started noticing girls and trying to impress them by acting grown-up or venturing further away from my neighborhood when playing and seeking new adventures.

We had hills, neighborhood streets, vacant lots, railroad tracks, and an extensive system of wide cemented ditches to play in and keep us occupied. Anyone who owned a bicycle could easily and quickly get to just about any place in town. Some even walked. I spent much time playing along the banks of the Mississippi River, flying kites from atop the levee, hitching rides back and forth across to the state of Mississippi on the ferry, and just looking for treasures along the banks.

With the help of my adventurous friends and intriguing surroundings, there was never a shortage of fun times. We lived in Helena, Arkansas, just a few blocks away from the banks of the Mississippi River in the Delta. It was a dream setting for any boyhood adventure.

In my preteen years, I spent much time playing in the hills around my house and neighborhood. The corner of Poplar and York Streets was a hot spot for kids my age. There were plenty of playmates to interact with, all within a block in any direction. We rode our bicycles and homemade soap box derby cars, played tag and kick-the-can, board games and mind games, shot our BB guns and slingshots, and just dreamed.

Just a block away, above us, was Reservoir Hill. In the summertime, it was covered with kudzu. Some kids call it "Kudzu Mountain." Kudzu is a vine that originated in Japan and China. In this country, it was initially discovered in Philadelphia at the 1876 World's Fair Centennial Exhibition. In the 1930s, it began to be widely planted all over the South to prevent soil erosion and help fight the Dust Bowl, which caused horrific agricultural damage. Now, it grows in every southern state. I've even seen it in Pennsylvania and understand it grows in Massachusetts, Michigan, and Nebraska.

Initially, planting kudzu was thought to be a solution to prevent soil erosion. However, that theory was false as it only grew high enough to hide the erosion.

In a sixty-day season, it can grow a foot a day. A 3-to-9-foot root base helps it store nutrients, making this possible. By 1998, kudzu had become so invasive that Congress officially placed it under the Federal Noxious Weed Act. We used to joke that we could hear it growing because it covered so much territory so fast. It is thick, deep, and sometimes bug-infested. It was impossible to play in or even attempt to hike through. In Helena, you can see it climbing trees, telephone poles, and even crossing over streets along the overhead wires and cables. It has no limits as it grows along borders, ditch banks, and many other areas. It will smother and kill shrubs, trees, and many other desirable yard plants when left unchecked. One can almost disappear when it grows across flat land while trying to walk through it. If growing on a hillside, stepping off over the end of the hill is possible because your footing is obscured. Thankfully, when we were kids, it became dormant in the winter months and died back to the point of almost disappearing. For a close-up look, it is still visible when visiting the Battery C Civil War Park in Helena. Fortunately, it is kept nicely trimmed away from the park.

Reservoir Hill was accessible, but we did not play there often in the summer months. The winter season and early spring presented a haven for any dream a kid could imagine on a playground. It overlooked probably fifty percent of Helena, looking east with direct views of the Mississippi River and the west shore of the state of Mississippi.

The entire downtown area of Helena was visible from the top of Reservoir Hill. We would dig caves, camp out, swing across a gulley on grape vines, hike, and watch the barges traveling up and down the river. Once in a while, we took snacks with us and watched the world go by. It was also a place for some kids to experiment with cigarettes without their parents' knowledge. The backside road provided access to the reservoir but was also a popular spot where lovers parked at night.

Reservoir Hill is the very end of Crowley's Ridge, a hilly geographical region covered with trees extending 200 miles north into Missouri from Helena. The east end of the hill was shaved down over the years to provide room for residential expansion. Some of that dirt was used to fill a creek that flowed to the river through the middle of early Helena. The most expansive ranging width of the ridge is roughly 12 miles, with the highest point only 150 feet. It looks higher because it rises out of the low, flat lands of the Delta.

One day, everything changed! It seemed we had lost our childhood innocence. I remember attending the Poplar and York Street hot spot to join the daily fun activities. Mrs. Cox, Dickie's mother, was in her front yard with several kids gathered around. Her words have lingered with me all of these years. "That awful thing," she said, referring to a coffin that had been unearthed with the body of a female in it on the "Hill." She wasn't referring to the body in the coffin. Her concern was that the glass face plate on the coffin had been broken, and toxic gasses might be released from the body, exposing kids to possible diseases.

It was my first up-close encounter with someone lying in a coffin. The body was in a state of decomposition due to the sudden exposure to air, but its distinguishing features were that of a young or middle-aged female still intact. I was left with an unforgettable memory of the sight!

I must have been traumatized because I do not remember any of the kids who were present. I know I wasn't alone because some friends I still have contact with say they saw it too. For the life of me, I can't recall my exact age at the time. I only remember the kudzu being dormant. Up to this point, we all were happy-go-lucky and free-spirited. I'm sure nothing this ghastly had ever occurred in our lives.

I do vividly recall that the coffin was hexagonal. It looked heavy and was made of rusty iron. The top consisted of an open hole, allowing the body's face and chest to be viewed. However, it was apparent that the opening should have been sealed with a glass insert because the broken glass was scattered over the corpse. It was also clear that the glass had been recently broken, causing the decay. The hexagonal shape of the rusty box was long, narrow, and tapered down to the feet. My next most vivid memory is that the body was a light brown-skinned. She appeared to be wearing a dress with fringes across the upper chest. It reminded me of a deer-skinned colored jacket with fringes seen in many American Indian museums. My initial impression was that the lady was wearing buckskins. For most of my life, I have wondered if she was an American Indian. My better judgment, though, is that the history of Helena did not present any American Indians that would have been buried in an iron box. These images have been burned into my brain for most of my life.

Sources:

wikipedia.org/wiki/Crowley's Ridge
wikihow.com/identify-kudzu

Chapter Two

LINGERING MEMORIES OF A COFFIN

The sight of my first dead body, especially in such a setting, has remained with me. I have told and retold the story many times over the years. The image of a female with long dark hair and brownish-colored skin wearing buckskins is a memory that will not leave my brain.

I have wondered what ever became of the person's remains for years. I remember discussing the story with people I grew up with, and to my surprise, many recall the incident or at least have heard the story. Some saw it, and others thought they had friends who had seen it.

As I grow older, I become more curious. I wondered who she was. How old was she? What year was she born? What year did she die? Did she die from a disease? What did she do during her life? Was she as young as I think she may have been? Why was she buried on our playground? Did she come from a wealthy family? What became of her and the coffin after we kids left the hill? Was she an American Indian or just dressed in Indian clothing?

Most importantly, the neighborhood parents did an excellent job keeping the kids away from Reservoir Hill while the authorities handled the situation. Their actions allowed time to pass while we grew older and put the shock and trauma behind us. The spread of kudzu during the summer provided an added cushion of time to forget the trauma because playing there was not an option during the summer months due to its dense growth.

As kids, we were never definitively told what the authorities did with the coffin. There were rumors it was reburied on the west side of the hill. Others say it was moved to a cemetery, probably Maple Hill. But moving it to another cemetery without knowing anything about this person seems unlikely. As we aged, we thought less and less about it and just kept being kids. We never saw evidence of it being reburied somewhere else on the hill.

In the golden years of my life, lingering memories and unanswered questions have grown, and I have to know more about my early childhood thoughts and wild speculations. So, with today's internet search engines, communications, archives, records, metal detectors, web pages, etc., I have made it my quest to solve this mystery.

With today's technology, reaching an easily documented conclusion should have been a slam dunk. But my searches and investigations have often been frustrating. The deeper I dig, the deeper I have found I have to dig! The phrase "looking for a needle in a haystack" doesn't even come close here. The problem is that there is no haystack.

Looking back 100 to 200 years is like walking through the woods and being blind. The state of Arkansas did not require birth or death certificates until 1914. So, that angle is a non-starter. If there are records like this available, I would need names and dates because they are privately held.

I started by discussing the event with some of my close friends from that era. It's incredible how some remember the event, but their recollections are different from mine. What's more impressive is that some have no mindfulness of it at all. Well, it's only been some seventy-plus or minus years, and I am still trying to figure out the problem! As a result, I have spent numerous months establishing a timeline as a starting point. This alone has been challenging. Our parents are deceased, and some of my friends are as well.

Initially, I thought it would be easy to pull up an article from the *Helena World* newspaper, reporting kids discovering a coffin with a body. But before this can be done, I must have a date or at least an approximate year. The closest I have come to the dates were between 1953 when I was ten years old, and 1958, when I was fifteen. I picked those years because I can recall other events during those periods. I've tried associating these events with the discovery, but no dots connect.

I have spent numerous, laborious, painful hours reviewing the *Helena World* microfilm covering 1953 through 1958 in the Arkansas State Archives Library. Found nothing! But this doesn't mean there is no article relating to the coffin because the microfilm is hard to read. It is distorted, blurry, and, in some places, cut off, unreadable, dark, and often out of focus. It's very tedious to view so much material in this condition. Microfilm is the only recorded opportunity still accessible to *Helena World*. Most other newspapers have had their information entered into the NewsPapers.com site operated by Ancestry. Their communication is accessible to click away at, especially if you have dates and names. Not so with the *Helena World*. Each paper page appears on microfilm; you must scan the entire page to find a related article. By contrast, NewsPapers.com is accessed by just entering one or several keywords with a proposed date and location.

In my first book, *Holly Street*, I spoke of Reservoir Hill and told the general story about the coffin. I also presented an article and picture taken from UPI telling a story of a coffin that looked just like the one we found as kids. The authorities may have taken it from the hill and dumped it into the Mississippi River as an easy way to solve the problem of not knowing how to handle it or where to place an unknown corpse. I made this connection because, in the 1940s or 1950s, it was common knowledge that the sheriff dumped slot machines from the ferry into the river as a solution to stop gambling. Here is an article describing a casket found on the Mississippi River bank.

> **Memphis, May 26 (UPI) – Rivermen have found a casket in the bank of the Mississippi River containing a skeleton, burial clothing, and a dime dated 1856. The barge crew which found it said the coffin would be turned over to the Memphis Museum.**

Capt. Morrison Warner of the motor vessel Caleb H. said the 200-pound casket was found Friday at the edge of the river on the caving banks of Island 62, about 82 miles south of Helena.

Warner said the casket was protruding from the river bank. He said his ship was bringing a tow of nine empty barges up River from Baton Rouge to Paducah.

"But we were curious when we saw the casket and put in to dig it out of the bank," Warner said. "It did not take us long, although it was more than half buried."

Warner said the coin had 13 stars in a circle.

The coffin had a glass covering on the lid, but the glass was broken. The opening is about 20 inches across, and the casket tapers from about 27 inches at one end to some 14 inches at the other end.

Warner said that clothing on the skeleton included a pair of shoes with two-inch heels. The shoes, which were in comparatively good condition, were estimated to be about size nine. Caleb H.'s crew left the coffin on a dock here and directed that it be offered to the Memphis Museum.

There is the possibility that the coffin could have been washed downstream from Helena and become stuck in the river bank. The article's date was May 26, 1958, and fits the broad timeline of when the coffin was found on Reservoir Hill. Considering and allowing time for it to wash down the river with the information I had, I may have overreacted by blaming authorities. They now cannot defend themselves, but this had to be investigated.

After numerous hours of searching for a picture like the coffin I remember as a kid, I posted one I found on *Facebook*. Several years ago, I remember watching the trendy TV show *Pawn Stars*, where someone offered a comparable coffin for sale that I had seen on Reservoir Hill. I began looking through many years of *Pawn Stars* TV shows on YouTube. Lo and behold, after hours and hours of searching, I found the coffin I remember. The only difference was this one has not been used and may be slightly differently shaped on the bottom.

In 1844, iron stove designer Almond Dunbar Fisk of New York acquired a patent on a stove capable of using wood or coal. He had partnered with his father-in-law Harvey Raymond in a small foundry business. For years, Fisk knew how to make airtight stoves and boilers and was interested in making an airtight iron coffin. He knew if the coffins were made in the body's shape, they would contain less air and minimize microorganisms that cause bacteria. Embalming still needed to be perfected, and refrigeration was unknown.

The most common Fisk coffin was manufactured in the years after 1848 and is similar to the one I saw as a kid. Depending on the eleven different sizes made, these sold from $6 to $25. As time progressed, airtight iron coffins with glass face plates increased from $100 to $300. Usually, only wealthy people could afford one, while wooden ones sold from $2 to $3.

So, eliminating air entry into the coffin would allow remains to be preserved from decomposition and enable them to be transported and protected from nature's elements, which would cause decay. Being airtight, it was also waterproof and provided sanitary protection from exposure to diseases such as yellow fever, smallpox, typhus, scarlet fever, and others prominent at the time. It became a boon for the coffin manufacturing industry. Shipping bodies long distances by rail back to family members for burial was almost impossible in a wooden coffin. Family members were now also able to view the body of their loved ones through the glass face plate.

In his design, Fisk consulted with Doctor Valentine Mott, a skillful New York surgeon with perfected dissection skills. Doctor Mott was also a collector of Egyptian mummies and had traveled to Egypt several times, acquiring knowledge of Egyptian sarcophagi. By November 1848, Fisk and Raymond had received their patent and manufactured Fisk Metallic Burial Cases. Because of their patent, I chose 1848 as my reference year to search for a possible identity.

Fisk also manufactured a very elaborate product, which received national acclaim when the former first lady, Dolly Madison, was laid out for public viewing in Washington, D.C., in 1849. Her coffin was one of the early designs imitating a sarcophagus.

Later that year, a fire destroyed the foundry and left Fisk searching for a way to restart his business. He offered his patent to John Forbes. Forbes was Harvey Raymond's brother-in-law, and Forbes' business partner was Horace White. Needing cash flow to restart the business, Fisk and Raymond entered into a deal with a stove manufacturing company in Cincinnati to continue the coffin business. A year later, Fisk died from lung problems he developed from the fire at the foundry. Through the subsequent years, the Fisk patent passed to the Cincinnati company, and they continued to manufacture coffins under the Fisk name and patent before new owners took over the company.

The word coffin comes from the Old French word 'cofin,' which means case or little box. The French word originated from the Latin word 'cophinus.' Later, it was called a coffer in Middle English before being named a coffin.

Today, coffin use is rare in the United States but still common in Europe. Not only is it a rarity, but the word coffin has become almost extinct because caskets have replaced them. Both the coffin and casket serve the same purpose. Of course, both are burial containers. Coffins are sometimes octagonal (8 sides) but generally hexagonal (6 sides). Caskets are rectangular (4 sides) and are typically fitted with a dividing cover/lid. The upper part of the lid is generally left open for viewing before burial. For a coffin, the entire top was made of one piece. Because of this, some were made with a glass face plate, which allowed viewing.

A coffin is narrower because it is anthropometrically constructed to fit the form of the human body by tapering down in size toward the feet. Caskets are more oversized but usually weigh less because they are made from lighter-weight material. Most Fisk coffins were made of heavy iron and usually weighed 200 to 300 pounds. My memory of the coffin I saw fit this description.

Coffins were mainly used in the Americas until around the 1880s for those who could afford one. The poorer families wrapped their deceased loved ones in blankets for burial. Caskets became better known and more used as the nineteenth century drew close. People began to feel that coffins were unrefined and, in some cases, suggested hints of creepy horror stories. The term casket seemed more socially acceptable as its appearance presented a perception of dignity and comfort as the final resting place. Regardless of perception or size, the shape is the main difference between a coffin and a casket.

I found information that confirmed my assumption and memory, explaining how the body I saw had been perfectly preserved for numerous years. *Gone to the Grave* by Abby Burnett describes the obituary of Mary Stewart Battles of Carroll County, Arkansas, in 1911. When Mary Stewart died, she had left instructions to be buried next to her late husband, who had died 49 years earlier in 1862. He was a Civil War soldier who died at Camp Wickliffe, Kentucky. His remains were embalmed and sealed in an iron coffin with a glass cover and returned to his home in Arkansas. Her deceased husband's brother exhumed his brother to make room for his sister-in-law to be laid next to him. The article reads:

> **When the body was removed Thursday, Tracy Battles, aged fifty-four of Chardon, expressed a desire to see his father, whom he had never known. The top of the casket was removed, and Mr. Battle gazed for the first time upon this father's face in a perfect state of preservation through the glass. The venerable Edwin Battles, the last of the family, viewed his brother's face Thursday and said: 'He looks just as he did the day we buried him.' Mrs. Melissa Richmond, the daughter, now fifty years old, also saw her father Thursday for**

> **the first time in her life. She had no childish memory of his face. The remains were apparently those of a person who had been dead for two days. The soldier's blanket was just as white as when wrapped around the body nearly a half-century ago. The skin, flesh, and hair were perfectly natural, the hair showing comb marks plainly. At the cemetery, many gazed upon the remarkable sight.**

I found a similar story initially published in *The News Star* from Monroe, Louisiana, in 1955, written by Yvonne Herron. Bonnie Bolden republished an updated version in the 125th-anniversary edition in 2016. Notice how people assumed the lady was Spanish because of her clothing and how the body began to decay when the glass was cracked. Also of interest is that the coffin resembles the fact it had to be constructed after 1848 because the woman would have been 53 years old, and the year would have been 1853 when she was buried.

> **On Feb. 3, 1955, workers laying a water line for a home on Lakeshore Drive hit a brick tomb enclosing a casket. The bricks, made of lime and sand, crumbled, and revealed an ornate cast-iron casket. Bob Bentz, for whose home the line was being installed, said the brick enclosure fell to pieces when struck by metal.**
>
> **He said after the casket was discovered; he thought the "only thing to do was take it to a funeral home since it couldn't be placed back in the same plot of ground. I called Hixson Brothers and asked that they remove the casket to the funeral home for reburial." Bentz said all parties acted on the advice of public health officials.**

Tom Mulhearn said in 1955 that type of casket was used primarily in New Orleans in the early 1800s, and this one was likely shipped here by boat.

The casket, approximately 6 feet long, measured 7.5 inches across at the foot. The widest part was 16 inches wide. It was decorated with ironwork and showed traces of black and orange paint. A cast-iron plate was fitted securely over a piece of glass on the front but removed after the body arrived at the funeral home. The glass clearly revealed a well-preserved, petite woman's body.

Accounts said the woman's features were exceptionally small. Near the face were magnolia blossoms and leaves, and the top of a black silk dress and a lace handkerchief were visible. Later in the day, the body's condition had considerably deteriorated because of a crack in the glass.

Hundreds visited Hixon Brothers until late Feb. 3 to view the spectacle. A 1976 story by Betty McMillan on local hauntings referred to the corpse as the Spanish Lady, noting a lace mantilla in the coffin.

The next day, under orders from the public health office, Monroe police were put on duty, and the casket was closed from public view. The parish health department ordered that the casket be reburied. Hixon Brothers Funeral Home buried the casket in an unmarked grave in Memorial Park Cemetery. The story posited that the lady's ghost roams where her body was found.

Who was she?
Benjamin Tennelle, who came here from either South Carolina or Georgia, was known to have lived in that area in the early 1800s and had a number of daughters. The property where the casket was found was known as Magenta Plantation.

Half of a silver plaque found on the casket bore the inscription "St. Clair Wade" and listed and age as either 30 or 39 years. The date, Sept. 7, 1814, was exceptionally clear. A capital "H" or "M" can be before the St. Clair but was not definite.

John Humble, who in 1955 was a well-informed local history authority, said records disclosed that a Mira St. John Tennelle, who married Hobert Hail, died about 1811. Another daughter, Jane St. Claire Tennelle had the same middle name as on the silver plate on the casket. Humble said that Jane St. Claire Tennelle was known to have been living in 1835 and was married to John Hughes.

Lora Peppers, who works in genealogy at the Ouachita Parish Public Library, said the "girl in the iron coffin" wasn't a Tennelle at all. Peppers, referencing "Founding Families of the Ouachita Valley" by Dr. E. Russ Williams, said the woman was Mary Catherine St. Clair Morrison Wade, born Sept. 17, 1814, and died at 39 years old.

Sources:
The Fisk Metal Burial Case by Ken Redman on Google
Crane & Breed Mfg. Co. on Google
A Brief History of the Fisk Coffin on Google, February 27, 2019
Allison Meier, December 30, 2013, Google
From Coffins to Caskets: An American History, Coffinworks.org
Coffins vs. Caskets: What's the Difference? Posted by Overnight Caskets 10/27/2021
YouTube *Pawn Stars* TV Show
United Press International (UPI) May 1958
Gone to the Grave by Abby Burnett
www.thenewsstar.com/story/news/local/2016/03/14/monroeyans-displayed-disinterred-corpse-55/81532682/

Chapter Three

BABY FORMULA FUND-RAISER

Covering all possible leads of my wild childhood speculations and curiosity has kept me open to any potential searches. Referring back to the *UPI* article in the previous chapter, I have continued to try to connect the idea that the coffin found south of Helena in 1958 in the Mississippi River could be the same coffin I saw as a kid. The shape of it was very similar to the one in my memory.

The resemblance of that coffin is very close to a previous image of the Fisk Coffin I found searching through archives of the TV show *Pawn Stars*. The view of the Fisk coffin was more like the rusty brown color of the one unearthed when I was a kid. The discovery of it in the river also piqued the interest of other news outlets. *The Commercial Appeal* provided more details reported about the barge company and other business owners along the river in Memphis. That information allowed more avenues of searching for answers.

Coffin Interest Lacking In City ---None Want It

There aren't many antique iron coffin fanciers in Memphis, it turned out yesterday.

Earl Eckman at Memphis Mid-Stream Service Co. said he had just one caller yesterday to see the iron coffin that crewmen of the Caleb H. extracted from the bank of the Mississippi River below Helena last week.

It was brought to Memphis and left at Mr. Eckman's dock at the foot of Beale in hopes that either the University of Tennessee or Memphis Museum might want it.

The only nibble was from a student at the U-T college of medicine, who said he'd like to have the skeleton inside.

"I wouldn't mind letting him have it," Mr. Eckman said, "but we'll keep it around a couple of days to see if a museum might want it."

The coffin is pretty old. A dime minted in 1856 was found in it.

The *Caleb H* riverboat transferred the coffin to another boat, the *Frankie & Johnnie,* four miles north of Memphis. Because *Caleb H* was pushing nine empty barges, it was safer and more accessible to transfer the coffin north of the Memphis harbor rather than risk clogging up the shipping lanes while trying to dock a boat pushing nine barges. *Frankie & Johnnie* then turned it over to Earl Eckman, owner of the Mid-Steam Service Company, which owned docks along the river. These people probably knew one another and did business together.

Coffin May Whet Diners' Appetites

Antique River Find Obtained By Lobster Shack

Connoisseurs of fine lobsters will be able to join in a wake when they dine at Pappy and Jimmy's Lobster Shack at 2100 Madison.

The antique iron coffin extricated from the Mississippi River bank below Helena last week was "sold" yesterday to the restaurant, which plans to put it on display with other relics of bygone days.

Earl Eckman, owner of Memphis Mid-Stream Service Co., let the coffin go for a $10 donation from the restaurant to the Cynthia Milk Fund of the Memphis Press-Scimitar.

Lehman C. 'Pappy' Sammons said a glass panel in the coffin would be replaced so diners could see the skeleton inside. He plans to leave it just as it is, corrosion and all.

"You can buy a shiny iron coffin from a mail order catalog. This one is special. We'll leave it just like it is."

The coffin is likely very old. A dime minted in 1856 was found with the skeleton, which appears to be the remains of a woman wrapped in a black shroud.

It was brought to Memphis by crewmen of the Caleb H, who found it. They thought a Memphis museum ought to have it for display.

The crew of the *Caleb H* must have anticipated that the coffin had some historical value because it looked nothing like the caskets of the day. Most of these articles referred to it as a casket, not a coffin. By this time, most people had availed themselves of the idea that the term coffin revealed a spooky, dreadful feeling. These same descriptions are still present when discussing death, burial, and caskets. Earl Eckman seemed to have found himself in a dilemma once he acquired the coffin. This article, from the May 26, 1958 edition of the *Memphis Press-Scimitar*, found him looking for a way to rid himself of the coffin. At the same time, he wanted to do the right thing and place it where people would enjoy seeing its historical value.

He Has a Casket—
And It's Occupied

Earl Eckman, owner of Memphis Mid-Stream Service Co., was wondering today what to do with an old cast iron casket with a skeleton inside it, left on his dock.

"I'd just as leave slide it back into the river where it came from," Eckman laughed.

But he held onto it because the river men who found it on Island 62 some 30 miles downstream from Helena, Ark., saw some historic value in it. Finders were the crew of the Motor Vessel Caleb H, which was bound upstream from Baton Rouge to Paducah, Ky. The river washed the casket out of the bank on Island 62. An old burial plot of the Civil War period had been lost to the meanderings of the stream.

According to the following article from *The Commercial Appeal,* dated May 27, 1958, Earl Eckman must also have thought that either the Memphis Museum or the University of Tennessee School of Medicine might find some use for the coffin's future. I assume the UT student may have wanted the skeleton as a study project, and maybe the Memphis Museum would place the coffin on exhibit.

In 1961, I attended Christian Brothers College in Memphis. Pappy and Jimmy's Lobster Shack was just a short distance away. I went there a couple of times with my parents when they visited. I'm sure I could not have afforded to eat there without someone else paying for the food. I would have also found something else on the menu that did not smell like lobster. I am not a fish eater because I find the fishy smell unpleasant. If the coffin with the skeleton was in the restaurant when I ate there, I'm glad I don't remember. That would have been a double dose of fetidness for my picky nose.

Through further investigation, I have determined that this coffin most likely washed up from one of the lowland cemeteries along the Mississippi River between Helena and Island 62. So, I have to apologize for my assumption that local authorities would have done something so outrageous as to dump a body in a coffin into the Mississippi.

Pappy and Jimmy's Lobster Shack added the coffin and displayed it with its many other oddities, artifacts, and antiques. However, I'm sure the coffin didn't belong there. I have always been taught that the human body is a temple of the Holy Ghost made in the image of God, so displaying it like this was irreverent.

I am glad Memphis had a way to prevent a baby formula shortage like the world experienced in 2022. Another article showed that Pappy & Jimmy's Lobster Shack paid Earl Eckman $10 for the coffin, which was to be donated to the Cynthia Milk Fund. I have no idea how long the restaurant kept the coffin on display or what may have become of it. At the time, it was a reminder for patrons to help support the organization.

The Cynthia Milk Fund originated in 1914 when a reporter named Memory McCord of the *Memphis Press* newspaper stumbled into a situation while completing an assignment. Her pen name was Cynthia Grey.

One cold winter night, she was assigned to cover a story about an accident in the poor section of downtown Memphis. She mistakenly knocked on the wrong door when she got to the area. As she realized the incorrect address and started to leave the apartment, she noticed a pile of rags in the corner moving. Under the rags was a malnourished, frigid baby near death. The child's mother explained she had three children, but the father, a good man, had contracted an incurable disease and could no longer work. The family was left without income, so the father took his own life to relieve some of the pressure so the rest of the family could live. After departing, Memory McCord arranged for a nearby drug store to deliver a quart of milk to the home daily for the rest of the month. She also wrote an article about the family's condition and asked for donations. Because of her awareness and compassion, the baby and the low-income family survived.

The *Memphis Press* took up the call for donations and established the Cynthia Milk Fund. By 1921, the fund provided milk, health care, food, and other necessary baby items. From 1926 through 1933, generous Memphians, through the Cynthia Milk Fund, supplied over 468,000 pints of milk for poor children.

The paper later changed its name to the *Memphis Press-Scimitar* and sponsored yearly fundraisers, which allowed it to grow and support low-income families with babies. The *Memphis Press-Scimitar* stopped publication in 1983, but *The Commercial Appeal* took over the fund.

Over the years, various businesses and charitable organizations have supported the Cynthia Milk Fund, keeping it at the forefront of needy low-income families with babies. On July 4, 1956, Elvis Presley even got into the act before 14,000 people in a sellout crowd at Russwood Park and donated all the proceeds to the Cynthia Milk Fund.

More than 100 years later, COVID-19 struck in 2019, causing nationwide shortages and affecting almost everything. By 2022, the lack of baby formula resulted in catastrophic hardships for young mothers. During this time, the Le Bonheur Children's Hospital provided "nurturing through nutrition" for babies by partnering with the Cynthia

Milk Fund. This joint effort helped many to weather the storm. Today, it continues to ensure a supply of lifesaving baby products.

Also, in 2022, *The Commercial Appeal* celebrated its 175th year of existence, which included the evolution of its different names, mergers, and acquisitions. As peculiar and irreverent as it was to display human remains in a restaurant in 1958, this tiny $10 exchange, as reported in the Memphis newspapers, played an essential part in the many donations that have kept the Cynthia Milk Fund in the forefront of being a worthwhile organization.

Sources:

Memphis Press-Scimitar
ElvisPresleymusic.com
The Best Times, G. Wayne Dowdy 12-1-2018
The Commercial Appeal

Chapter Four

LEARNING THE LANDSCAPE

Helena was a thriving community in the 1950s. The downtown area was bustling with businesses and shoppers. It was a great place to live if you were a teenager, especially if you had access to a car. Many restaurants, hotels, five-and-dime stores, and other specialty shops existed. Nichols Printing Company's specialty was all things printed, including repairing typewriters. My Uncle Joe did this work. It was routine for a novice with a typewriter to jam up the keys and virtually render it unusable. Since there were no computers, the typewriter was the most sophisticated machine for the ordinary person to write or create records. When I went off to college, I acquired a Smith-Corona typewriter. I soon learned it was less efficient than the simple pencil and paper, so I hardly ever used it. Also, there was no spell-check feature!

Gist Music Company was established in 1933. It sold 33 RPMs, the latest 45s listed in the top 10 for only a dollar. Although out of business today, Gist still displays musical instruments behind its shuttered store windows. Lately, I have information that someone is interested in reopening it. Although a small part of the revitalization of Helena, this is excellent news.

The biggest attraction of downtown was the main street, Cherry Street, which ran parallel to the Mississippi River. It also contained two movie theaters and four drug stores, with one having a soda fountain reminiscent of the paintings done by Norman Rockwell. Several clothing and shoe stores filled the gaps, including a hardware store, a furniture store, and a new Ford car dealership. A Chevrolet dealer was located in the same area.

Before the "big box store," there was a Sears Roebuck and Montgomery Ward store on Cherry Street. These stores weren't locally owned but franchises. Shopping inside them was possible, but if you needed something they did not have, all you had to do was look in a furnished company catalog and order it. Unlike today's Amazon, it took weeks to receive your order.

It's hard to believe that Helena once had numerous little "mom-and-pop" stores all over town. They specialized in groceries, but each also provided a signature item such as cigarettes, alcohol, or ice cream. My grandfather sold 22 shells and a variety of fresh meats. As a kid, I was more familiar with them than my friends because I helped my father on his bread route. Off the top of my head, I can recall at least 25 businesses. These little stores were scattered in different sections all across town. Most kids I grew up with were unaware of the many other neighborhoods that made up Helena. The stores were owned by people with living quarters attached to the back of them. Some were openly exposed to the store, so customers could come in late and make a purchase.

Almost every store contained a glass-paneled refrigerator displaying meats, primarily cold cuts, and other perishables. These giant "meat counters," as they were called, were usually in the back of the store. Behind the meat counter, the grocer had a butcher block where he would cut up each order for a customer with a cleaver. There were very few individual packages of processed meat products. Things like bacon, steaks, and pork chops were cut from large slabs purchased from a distributor and then sold to the customer by the pound. Electronic scales were nonexistent. The correct weight was determined by hand-sliding individual metal weights until they were balanced.

Some stores had a second refrigerator that contained sodas, beer, and milk. Very few could afford a freezer. The other products, like bakery and canned goods, were kept on shelves along the walls. It was a tricky business for these small stores; none of the owners got rich. They had difficulty scratching out a living because the profit margin was tight.

They served regular customers living within a block or two with similar incomes as the store owners. People desiring more variety than the small mom-and-pops sold shopped at Safeway, Joe's Super Market, or Watkins.

The Phillips County Court House was on the north end of Cherry Street at the corner of Perry Street, where a statue of the WWI Doughboy stood. It was installed and dedicated in 1927 for $2,065, with money raised by the Phillips County Memorial Association. The association started in the 1800s, after the Civil War, and raised money to build and support monuments honoring Confederate soldiers from Arkansas. After WWI, most of the memorial committee members were getting old and preferred to use the raised money to aid the Confederate Cemetery. Younger members favored honoring WWI veterans with a statue like the Doughboy found installed in several other cities nationwide. The Doughboy inspired the committee members and approved it with a 100% vote.

In the 1950s Cherry Street was the hot spot for teens to demonstrate their wheels by making the drag (driving their cars from one end of the street to the other by making a U-turn on each end and repeating the process). It extended for seven blocks circling the Doughboy, which was placed in the middle of the street on the north end, then back to Nicks Café, located dead center on the south end. The levee stood directly across from Nicks. The train depot was sandwiched between it and the café. This levee area contained a cement sea wall with a narrow opening, which provided access to the Mississippi River car ferry.

Teens paraded back and forth on Cherry Street, making the drag. It was no problem if cars stopped to converse with another carload of teenagers traveling in the opposite direction. Everyone was having a good time socializing and trying to make a big impression on others of the opposite sex while their young hormones raged. And, of course, there was always a guy making a spectacle with his souped-up loud car equipped with a set of glass pack mufflers. The decibels were earsplitting once he put his foot on the gas pedal. Some teens tried to make others believe they drove an air-conditioned car by keeping the windows rolled up in the summer months before air conditioning was widely available.

The drag action started every day after school and continued throughout the weekend. Most stores were open on Saturdays until 9 p.m. as Cherry Street rocked on well after dark.

Teens also had several other places of entertainment while gathering with their friends after dark, particularly on weekends. The Inn-B-Tween-Drive-Inn featured a car hop service. Some of us even ordered beer without getting our I.D. checked. The Kreme Freeze offered excellent ice cream delights and specialty fountain floats. The Half-Way-House was another favorite spot featuring great hamburgers and finger foods. Most of these places were always packed with carloads of teenagers just hanging out and having fun. It was an opportunity for kids from the different schools in Phillips County to meet. Everyone either knew one another or at least knew who was who. If you had a crush on someone, it was a self-kept secret to move from place to place until you spotted your heartthrob. Once in a blue moon, turning up a new one amongst all the excitement and fun was possible.

The Teen Club was also a unique spot favored by many. It was open for teenagers on Friday and Saturday nights and was overseen by Mrs. Robinson. She was a wonderful lady with much patience, which made a difference. She provided a gathering place where teens could stay out of trouble and knew all of us by name. The club was equipped with a dance floor, and we had an assortment of all the latest rock and roll records. Some teenagers played ping pong, while others sat in booths, visited, and played cards or other games. I loved to arm wrestle, and the booths were ideal for facing my opponent. Once a month, Mrs. Robinson hired one of the local bands made up of high school students. She only charged 50 cents for admission. There was no charge for the other weekends. These were some of the best nights because many kids from the different hang-outs usually attended, creating opportunities to meet and dance with new people.

The financial district was also well established, with the Phillips National Bank on the corner of Rightor and Cherry and the Helena National Bank just down a few blocks south. A couple of savings and loan companies were also in town. Sandwiched on the second-floor building on York Street was the KFFA radio station, which started broadcasting the King Biscuit Radio Show in 1941. It still airs today and can lay claim to be one of the country's longest-lasting radio programs.

The downtown section of Helena consisted of more than just Cherry Street. On Missouri Street, there were two bus stations, Beith Bus Line and Brocato Bus Line, which were within one block of another but served different routes in opposite directions.

Walnut Street ran parallel one block over to the west. It also contained a movie theater and several African American honky-tonks, frequently called juke joints. The Albert Ragsdale Cities Service station was at the end of the block across the street from Keeshan-Lambert Funeral Home. Sanders Buick dealership, which sold its fair share of automobiles, was on the next block north and catty-cornered from the John Deere Tractor dealership. A bit further south stood Watkins Supermarket, known for its meats. Webb Meat Packing Company was located on the next block and distributed to all area stores.

I can't leave out Messina's Liquor Store, which is still in business today. Mr. Messina was my great-uncle by marriage to my grandfather's sister. I had no problem going into the store when I was underage and making a purchase. Uncle Charlie would look the other way when I told him I was 21. We both knew better! I never knew of any retail establishment in the fifties that was ever busted for selling alcohol to a minor. It was a way of life in Helena then, and everyone knew it!

The biggest open secret, though, was Yazoo Street. It was just one block long on the south end of downtown, with several houses with red porch lights turned on at night. Before I was even a teenager, I remember seeing migrant Mexican laborers lined up on Saturday nights in front of these houses. Today, only two are left standing but are closed for business. Even though the street signs have been removed, visitors can only locate Yazoo Street with a GPS or directions given by an "old timer."

Helena even had its own local Coca-Cola bottling plant and, at one time, shared space with its competitor, Dr. Pepper. Local bottling plants were located all over the country. Each plant provided its' own glass Coke bottles displaying the city's name pre-engraved on the bottom.

The empty bottles could be returned for credit for two to ten cents each. The local companies washed, cleaned, and rebottled them with the secret Coke formula. Collecting engraved Coke bottles with a city name was a big deal. Every kid I knew had an assortment of engraved bottles. It was like collecting baseball cards. The Coca-Cola Company stopped using glass years ago when plastic bottling became prevalent and less costly. I wish I had kept my collection!

Habib's bakery on Cherry Street also made and sold various pastries, cakes, and pies. They were famous for their fruit cakes and shipped them worldwide in tin cans. My friend, Bobby, told me he still has one of these cans. A great piece of memorabilia!

My Aunt Dorothy ran the Royal Bakery on the corner of Rightor and Pecan Streets. She began at 4 a.m. daily making delicious deep-fried donuts and other pastries. I remember she sold the donuts for "a nickel apiece or five for a quarter." Poor people used to flock in early to buy the donuts. The tax was one cent beginning on the first 25-cent purchase. If someone wanted more than five donuts, they would buy the first four. In a separate purchase, they would accept any additional number of up to four again to save a penny in taxes. I remember teasing Aunt Dorothy about this because it annoyed her. She was also acclaimed for making tiered wedding cakes and selling various flavored ice creams packed into cones. In the 1940s, my father and Uncle Tripp operated their bread routes from the bakery, which baked and wrapped Town Talk brand bread. Their routes covered all of Helena, most of Phillips County, and parts of other nearby counties.

During these years, Helena had an average population of 10,000 to 12,000. Even though small, it was very dynamic with its modest businesses, keeping its citizens employed, fed, housed, and clothed. Later, it was a bonus when a couple of large plants opened in West Helena and provided even more jobs. For example, I remember Bobbie Brooks Dress Factory, Mohawk Rubber Company, and Doughboy Plastics.

Helena has always been the largest town in Phillips County, so it's hard to believe Poplar Grove, with a population of 400, was the second-largest community in 1873. In the 1950s, its recorded population could have been more noticeable. But, like many other similar small centers in the county, the young residents gathered at the teen club and participated in Little and Pony League baseball. It was 17 miles west of Helena on the Arkansas Midland Railway Line and was a thriving center for the surrounding farmers.

A hundred years earlier, this little place had a post office, six general stores, four churches, a saw-mill, two blacksmiths' shops, one livery stable, two hotels, a cotton gin, two schools (one for Blacks and one for Whites), and an undertaker. Most of those establishments no longer remained in my early years, but many families still sparsely populated the countryside.

Farming was the top industry in Phillips County. Tons and tons of cotton were grown in the many miles surrounding Helena. Once picked, it was brought into town to be ginned and baled. The bales were shipped primarily by train to cloth manufacturing companies nationwide. Until the mid-1950s, Helena was surrounded by forests with large hardwood trees. Several decades earlier, the forest industry harvested these trees by hand. As mechanization advanced, more and more trees were removed and sold for lumber all across the world.

However, times changed across the state by 1955. Cotton remained king, but the poultry industry was now second place as a leading source of agricultural income in Arkansas.

Today, rice is the state's largest crop, and Arkansas is the nation's leading producer. Corn, wheat, and soybeans have surpassed cotton production as of 2022. But, poultry is the largest agricultural industry in the state, providing almost 158,000 related jobs.

The Recreation Park occupied an ample green space on the north end of town with picnic tables scattered under giant shade trees. Across the street, there were tennis courts, the Pony League, and Little League baseball parks. In the 1930s and 1940s, the Pony League Park was home to the Helena Seaporters, a minor league member of the Cotton States League. It was comprised of several teams from across the South. The best part of this park, though, was the swimming pool. It was designed for swimmers of all ages but not all colors. The older kids could swim in the 9-foot section and enjoy diving off a high dive or a low diving board, while the younger ones could play at the opposite end in the chest-high water. There was even a separate pool, called the baby pool, for toddlers and people who just wanted to sit in the water, covering their legs. All major religious denominations were well represented in Helena, including a large Jewish population with a beautiful temple built in 1912. The Catholic Church, with a large congregation, was built in 1935. It was famous for the behind-the-altar mural painted by Charles Quest and stained-glass windows designed by Emil Frei. We were told the extraordinary pieces of blue-tinted glass were only found in two other churches worldwide. And my parents were the first couple to get married there in 1936. The Baptist, Methodist, and Episcopal churches also filled their pews every Sunday. Religion and faith were more of an obligation requiring regular attendance than they are today.

Catholic students could begin Sacred Heart Academy for kindergarten and continue all grades through senior high. A few protestants were allowed to fill in the required class numbers. Central High offered only grades nine through twelve because all their students were assembled from several grade schools in both Helena and West Helena. The African Americans attended Eliza Miller due to segregation. It was located right below Reservoir Hill on its south side.

The government funded the public schools through taxes. Before the Civil War, there were no state-sponsored schools in Arkansas. I attended Sacred Heart Academy, and I remember that my parents paid tuition for my brother, myself, and my sister. I don't know the exact amount, but I recall taking a small kraft pocket-sized envelope containing a few dollars to give to the nuns about once a quarter. I thought it unfair that my non-Catholic friends attended school for free when my parents had to pay.

I used to have a couple of African American friends when I lived on Holly Street in the 1940s, just before I moved to College Street. Holly Street is a part of Helena, better known as North Helena. The majority of the population in the area were African Americans and, for the most part, poor. Once I moved to College Street, all my friends were White. I had forgotten most of my early childhood Black buddies.

Reservoir Hill was one of the most popular and fun places for boys to play and hang out. I don't recall ever seeing any African American kids on the Hill. We had fun just being up there looking over the city and letting our imaginations run at all speeds and in all directions. The area below, around Eliza Miller, was called Catholic Hollow. Only African-American kids played or lived in this area. If they didn't live there, they most likely went home after school to North Helena, where most other African Americans resided.

We knew part of the Battle of Helena had occurred there almost one hundred years earlier. Most of us didn't even know why the Civil War was fought. We all knew the South had lost, so that gave us cause to feel hurt about our Southern pride. I certainly wasn't going to let my Southern pride succumb to a Yankee victory.

I had no idea how much blood, guts, and body parts had been shed and scattered over the area almost ninety years earlier. The closest thing in my young mind was watching a cowboy and Indian movie at the Saturday matinee playing in the Malco. Watching someone being killed was only seeing them fall off their horse and slowly roll over and close their eyes. Our culture, as kids, was very sheltered.

Sources:

Mydeltaworld.com
Civilwaronthewesterrnborder.org
visitHelena.com
Goodspeed Publishing Company, *History of Phillips County Arkansas*
Phillips County Historical Quarterly Vol 17 No.1
Washington County Historical Society Collection
Shiloh Museum of Ozark History
Farm Bureau Arkansas, www.arfb.com

Chapter Five

Playground, Battleground, or Burial Ground?

As I write this book, I search for clues and answers. I am not an expert in uncovering records; however, I am learning as I progress. Also, without help from friends and interested parties, my story would have hit a dead end long ago. It's not easy to discover what became of a body some seventy-plus years ago, especially when it may have already been dead for one hundred years, and your primary source is memory. Thank goodness my memory is not the only one available to me.

I have learned so far that Reservoir Hill was initially named Graveyard Hill, and most of it was owned by individuals in the first half of the 1800s. Among the rolling hills, a short distance west of downtown Helena, lies the historic Battery C, one of four Civil War Union Army fortifications. For many Helenians, this site is more than just a Civil War Battery. It was, and most likely still is, the final resting place of many of the earliest pioneers of Helena. This hill was the settlement's earliest graveyard, untouched by kudzu and erosion.

Little has been written about Graveyard Hill. Most of what is known came after the Civil War when it was renamed Reservoir Hill. We knew individuals owned the hill (including Fleetwood Hanks, who built Estevan Hall). At times, the owners allowed early citizens to bury their dead on the Hill due to the flooding of the lower area around Helena.

Hanks, an early wealthy settler, started building his home in the 1820s. It may be the oldest standing building in Phillips County and has been passed down to descendants. The house, Estevan Hall, has been on the National Register of Historic Places since 1974. As of 2023, it's not open to the public. It is owned by Southern Bancorp Community Partners and is being renovated to be the future Civil War Helena Visitor Center.

By 1815, most of the earliest pioneers lived along Sterling Road, which ran parallel to the Mississippi River. Many of these pioneers and others arriving in the area began to build and dwell in what we knew as Old Helena. As cholera, yellow fever, malaria, and other diseases occurred, the locals started to use the hill as the settlement's graveyard. At the time, the hill must have been beautiful as it overlooked the small town and the river, giving the mourners left behind a sense of peace knowing their loved ones had been interred safely in such a lovely location. Although I recall seeing a light brown-skinned female in the coffin, she was not Black. I doubt the Southern culture would have permitted any dark-skinned people to be buried on Graveyard Hill.

However, all that peace and tranquility vanished in 1862 – 1863, when the Union Army built a rather large fortification on this hill. It was one of the four planned fortifications surrounding the city. Still, its location was critical, and the firing of artillery blew trees apart, dislodged large portions of the hill, and annihilated tombstones. With few trees left, erosion was inevitable, and this destruction and deterioration would eventually wholly destroy the cemetery portion of Graveyard Hill.

There is no mention in the existing literature of Graveyard Hill between the Civil War and 1869. Only limited information is found describing what happened to the already interred. However, by 1869, the citizens knew something had to be done. Some metal coffins were partially uncovered and had washed into the gullies formed by erosion. Wooden coffins had disintegrated, and headstones lay in pieces all around. Then, the Memorial Committee was formed to build a new cemetery.

The 1870 deed record book lists Henry P. and Eliza Coolidge, Henry C. and Bettie Rightor, and Albertis and Fannie Wilkins selling land containing seventy-three acres to Evergreen Cemetery Company for $13,500 on the city's north side. A superintendent was hired, and by December 1870, the City Council voted to bury paupers in the new cemetery. City ordinance 436 lists a drayage charge of $13.40, payable to the city to bury a pauper in the cemetery. I'm unable to find any records of who paid the pauper fees.

The minutes of the July 1879 city council meeting refer to "Potter's Field" as located in the cemetery. Whether or not this is about the paupers and where they were buried inside Evergreen Cemetery is still being determined.

As for those buried on Graveyard Hill, many were reinterred in Evergreen Cemetery (later called Maple Hill Cemetery in 1898). James M. Hanks, son of Fleetwood Hanks, wrote in his diary in October of 1872, "All of the dead buried in the family cemetery on the hill just north of his ancestral home was reburied in the Hanks lot in Evergreen Cemetery." Many others also reinterred family members in Evergreen Cemetery. A total of seventy-four headstones in Maple Hill denoted those who had been reburied from Graveyard Hill during the latter part of the 1800s. The names of those who died before 1865 and were reinterred can be found in *Phillips County Historical Quarterly*, Volume 3, #1, pages 21 – 26.

For those not reburied in Evergreen Cemetery, it's speculation about what became of those not listed. The online cemetery site Findagrave.com lists fifteen graves in Graveyard Hill. Some of these men were casualties of the Civil War and were probably reinterred in the Confederate Cemetery. Others are detailed but have yet to be verified as being reinterred. Findagrave.com refers to a letter dated April 30, 1854, written by David Garretson, the youngest son of Mason and Betsy Hardin Garretson, wherein he says he visited the grave sites of the Garretson family on Graveyard Hill in Helena, Arkansas. He mentions locating the graves of both parents, his sister Mary Garretson Powell, "the babe" (presumed to be Mary's unnamed baby), and Sarah Ann Garretson. Reburial for these ancestors has never been found or mentioned elsewhere, so it is assumed they remain buried among the ruins of Graveyard Hill or are part of the bodies washed into the gullies and covered with mounds of eroded topsoil.

A bit of information I have found most interesting shows that John Bruce Clay (1773-1829) was buried on Graveyard Hill. His home was in New Orleans, and while traveling back on the Steamboat *Rover,* he died about 20 miles south of Memphis. Findagrave.com lists his burial to be on Graveyard Hill in Helena. No other published files verify where his remains were interred.

I bring up John Bruce Clay because of his family ties. He was the brother of Henry Clay, the former Speaker of the U. S. House of Representatives, a U.S. Senator from Kentucky, and the ninth United States Secretary of State. He also ran for president in 1824, 1832 and 1844. He was known as "The Great Compromiser" because he possessed outstanding negotiation skills. Historians credit him for delaying the outbreak of the Civil War during the first half of the 19th century.

I can't verify actual records that the body of John Bruce Clay was allowed to be laid to rest on Graveyard Hill because of his influential family ties. Still, knowing the difficulties of transporting the dead during this era due to decomposition and the fear of diseases, it made sense to expeditiously inter Mr. Clay. Even wealth and influence made no difference in his death. He most likely was laid to rest in a wooden box, which, over time, most likely disintegrated. In 2023, I visited the prior estate of Henry Clay in Lexington, Kentucky, and spoke with one of the docents about John Bruce Clay. He seemed puzzled and didn't have any knowledge about the brother of Henry Clay.

Even after embalming became prevalent in 1861, many states passed laws requiring guidelines for transporting a corpse. A Transit Permit and a Certified Copy of the Death Record were required in most states. They had to be accompanied by the Certificate of Undertaker prepared by the State Licensed Embalmer. A Transit Label also needed to be completed by the undertaker, and it had to display each road, route, and point of transfer or connecting line from the point of origin to the final destination. The Transit Label document was required to be securely fastened to the end of the box containing the coffin, and it needed to be personally handed over to the escort.

The State of Mississippi mandated the box containing the coffin be constructed of tongued and grooved wood of not less than seven-eighths of an inch thick, with all joints put on with cleats or cross pieces, tightly closed with white lead, and coated with asphalt varnish or paraffin paint. A rubber gasket was also required between the casket's lid and the outer box.

If death was caused by smallpox, plague, Asiatic cholera, yellow fever, typhus fever, diphtheria, scarlet fever, erysipelas, anthrax, or leprosy, the body had to be thoroughly embalmed. All orifices were to be closed with absorbent cotton and washed with a disinfectant fluid. The body was to be placed into a metal coffin immediately and be hermetically and permanently sealed.

Every state had a variety of rules. New York allowed 60 hours of transportation, requiring the orifices to be closed with absorbent cotton, while Mississippi approved only 30 hours. The coffin's length also determined the number of handles that needed to be attached.

The coffin unearthed when I was a kid may be one of those left behind. It shocked us because we had no idea our playground had previously been a burial ground. Our parents were unaware of this, and, to my knowledge, none of the previous generation was aware of it being a cemetery. If they did, they never spoke of it. Everyone seemed surprised and confused.

My research reveals that over 70 bodies were moved to Evergreen Cemetery in 1872, which was approximately 80 years earlier than when our coffin was unearthed in the 1950s. The passage of this much time allowed this part of history to fade away. So, discovering a dead body where children were playing was new news. Most people living in Helena today are, as I was seventy years ago, unaware Reservoir Hill was ever a burial ground.

Everyone knew the Civil War Battle of Helena took place on Reservoir Hill and several other spots in the town. The problem was that none of us had ever heard of it referred to as Graveyard Hill. The size of it spread over several acres, giving us the freedom to stretch our imaginations beyond limits. The far east end of the hill is a cliff where the coffin was found. We spent most of our time in this area. After all, overlooking the city with an almost panoramic view was exhilarating for everyone. I spent hours flying my kite up there, and several of us camped just a few feet from where the coffin was unearthed. My friend Jimmy and I dug a cave inside the cliff, just a few feet below where the coffin was buried. Because of these vivid memories, I am obsessed with solving this mystery.

In addition to relocating the coffin and verifying that it is the same one I remember as a kid, I now have some adult dreams I would like to complete. First, I want to see this person appropriately buried in a marked grave. My other big goal is to have her buried on the hill in the center of Battery C, enclosed in a decorative fence protecting the grave, similar to the body of Petit Jean as displayed in Petit Jean Mountain State Park near Morrilton, Arkansas. It would be a place of honor for this person as a final resting place, telling her story, which could be shared with visitors, historians, and all who respect the value of life.

While no one is certain what happened to the rest of the bodies not reburied in Evergreen Cemetery, most are reasonably confident that Graveyard Hill, now covered in trenches and kudzu, remains the final resting place of some of the earliest pioneers.

Sources:

The above description, with permission, is copied from a post of *Reflections of the Past* by Patricia Ann Smith, *Facebook*
Biographical and Historical Memoirs of Eastern Arkansas, Goodspeed Publishing Company
Phillips County Historical Quarterly, Vol 3 No 1
Diaries of Judge James M. Hanks
Findagrave.com
deltabyways.com
Maple Hill Cemetery public information

tcgs.genealogyvillage.com
Findagrave.com, memorial 197656824
en.wikipedia.org, Henry Clay
Mississippi State Board of Health, June 25, 1926
Keeshan-Lambert Funeral Home Helena AR 1881-1956
Helena On the Mississippi Facebook page

Chapter Six

A NEW CITY

The first communities established near Helena were towns or villages surrounding the mouth of the St. Francis River, between the Mississippi River and Crowley's Ridge. The first of these settlements, Utica, is thought to have been developed close to the ridge, at the mouth of the St. Francis River, between 1803 and 1805. The first statewide mention of this town was in 1819, in the first issue of the *Arkansas Gazette.* According to the paper, this ancient town had one hundred residents. It was called old in 1819, and a gentleman named McLain owned a tavern on the island close to the mouth of the St. Francis River. In *Pioneers and Makers of Arkansas,* Josiah Shinn states, "Utica was a flourishing town of some possibilities in 1819, but gave place in time to the greater glory of Helena." Records reveal that many marriages were performed at Utica, and many Arkansans date their origins to this early village. In the same neighborhood, at a later date, was the town of Shirley, but it soon faded away with the growth of St. Francis (Helena). Early maps show Utica as a settlement but not St. Francis. However, by 1827, St. Francis had earned a place on state maps.

Utica's growth around 1817 was due to people awaiting the results of the first survey of the area. They had old Spanish Land Grants, military land warrants, New Madrid certificates, or certificates of purchase from the United States Government. In 1817, Utica was laid out as a town by Nicholas Rightor. Land boundaries were set, and settlers knew where their property lines were drawn for the first time. It is thought Nicholas

Rightor gave the name Utica, as he was from nearby Cooperstown in New York with the same name.

While the town of Utica was declining by 1830, works were underway to develop a new community called Sterling at the mouth of the St. Francis River, where it emptied into the Mississippi. It is difficult to determine the exact lifespan of this settlement. Postal records show it was a post office as early as 1848 and was discontinued as such in 1866. Maps of 1845, 1860, and 1888 account for Sterling as a town. However, a map from the 1878 Department of the Interior shows the mouth of the St. Francis River as a settlement but not named Sterling. It is believed the Martin family developed the plans for this community, as tax rolls catalog several related Martin families owning lots and acreage in Sterling from 1840 to 1850. Sterling was platted as a town site with lots to be sold. Lot numbers went as high as 585 in 1849—initially, lots sold from $10.00 an acre to $50.00 an acre. By 1850, the $10.00 lots had dropped to $3.00 and the $50.00 lots to $8.00. Unimproved lots varied from $10.00 to $67.00 per acre, while improved lots ranged from $100.00 to $600.00.

Whether Sterling was started as a place to benefit from the steamboat or lumber trade in the area has yet to be discovered. As late as the beginning of the Civil War, there were many woodyards and stave-making groups in the area.

In those days, it's understandable that many of these parts along the Mississippi River consisted of lowlands, swamps, and forests. However, I found how many bears inhabited some of these regions curious. I grew up hunting there but never saw any signs of a bear. No one I remember ever discussed the possibility of bears being around. Abundant deer, squirrels, and ducks were the targeted game in my youth between the 1940s and the 1960s. Coon hunting was also popular. Today, deer hunting is the most popular sport and was then, too. Remarkably, bear biologists estimated that the bear population of Arkansas was around 50,000 in the early 1800s, and Arkansas was often referred to as the "Bear State." Many hunters owned packs of trained bear hounds. One location near Modoc just south of Helena became a favorite spot for bear hunters from other states. These hunters would arrive by steamboat loaded with tents, supplies, and all necessary gear to participate in hunting bears for several days. A bear skin rug was quite the trophy! Sometimes, the hides were tanned to make shoes, clothing, or blankets, and the bear grease was used for various skin ailments such as rashes. A story I read tells of a group of hunters from Kentucky killing 32 bears in a single day. For some sportsmen, coming to the Arkansas wilderness was like going on an African safari.

By 1940, only 50 bears remained in the entire state. Now, approximately only 5,000 bears live in Arkansas because they are descendants of the 256 that the Game and Fish Commission imported from the Great Lakes area between 1958 and 1968.

Bear hunting has again become popular but is rigidly regulated. A regular license and a bear permit are required. The bear permit is free for Arkansas residents but costs $300 for nonresidents. In 2023, 765 bears were reported killed in Arkansas.

Times, though, have changed. Now, these lowland locations are heavily populated with wild boar. It's estimated that more than 200,000 boars reside in Arkansas. Hunting is regulated but more relaxed than it is for bears. They are a menace for farmers because they can uproot their crops. They are referred to as feral hogs, travel in large packs of sometimes up to 30, and will attack if threatened. A human cannot outrun one! So, a hunter could become the hunted under various circumstances. A few years ago, I traveled on the Low Road, and an estimated 20 boars crossed the road in front of my truck. A group of young pigs is called a litter, while a group of hogs is called a passel or team. Even more surprising is that a group of swine is called a sounder. Go figure! I would prefer they be called Arkansas Razorbacks. Studies have determined that 66% of the boars must be eliminated yearly to maintain a constant population.

County Court records make several references to the start of trade at Sterling. Joseph Wallen petitioned the Court in 1845 for a license to keep a public ferry across the Mississippi River from Sterling. In 1844 and 1845, individuals were granted several permits to keep grocery, retail, and vinous spirits shops. The 1840s were the years in which Sterling seemed to prosper.

It was quite a village off the Low Road at the juncture of the St. Francis and Mississippi Rivers. I remember my father taking us there to water ski in my preteen years. He had a nine-foot aluminum boat powered by a ten-horsepower outboard motor. It would fly! We would only dare venture past the mouth of St. Francis into the mighty Mississippi if we were cautious of water moccasins swimming around in St. Francis.

Baker Sparkman, whom many will remember from the 1960s, stated his grandmother planted Cedar trees at her home in the middle of the town. One of those trees stood across from the Mississippi River State Park signage for several years. Much of that town has now cascaded into the Mississippi.

Someone wrote, "Not long ago, an old swing attached to a tree in the pecan orchard was found. Rumor had it that the ghost of a little girl could be seen swinging at dusk. As the years passed, fellow citizens replaced the swing to accommodate the little girl. The swing was removed when the Mississippi River Park took over."

While Utica flourished, the settlement of St. Francis (Helena) also expanded. Sylvanus Phillips and W.B.R. Hornor had moved to St. Francis, as had others who had lived in Utica during the early years. No one is certain when the name changed from St. Francis to Helena, but by 1821, the name Helena was officially supplanted in the *Arkansas Gazette*, and the new name remained.

W.B.R. Hornor arrived in Helena in 1811 and was the first Hornor to reside in Arkansas. The Hornor name has produced many descendants who held prominent positions and accounted for the growth and development of Helena. However, according to the *Historical Sketch of the Hornor Family, since 1683*, W.B.R. Hornor has not left any direct descendants in Arkansas. The many Hornors that have resided and descended from the Helena Hornors began around 1836 and traced their heritage back to Judge John Sidney Hornor, nephew of W.B.R. Hornor, and wife Elizabeth Johnson, the daughter of Joseph Johnson, governor of Virginia. W.B.R. Hornor died in 1838.

Thanks to the efforts of W.B.R. Hornor, on May 1, 1820, this area of the Arkansas Territory was divided into the counties of Phillips, Lee,

Monroe, St. Francis, and parts of Crittenden. Before these years, this area had previously belonged to the Kingdom of Spain and then the Empire of France. Because settlers and France and Spain were calming the land, ownership was sometimes contentious.

Prior to 1800, both Spain and France claimed parts of the area. France laid their claims based on La Salle's exploration in 1682, and Spain made their claims based on Hernando de Soto's exploration in 1541. France ceded their area back to Spain after the French and Indian War, but Spain returned it to France in 1800.

In 1803, the United States acquired the area from France, which was known as the Louisiana Purchase. Then, in 1805, Congress passed legislation establishing legitimate rules and procedures for proper land ownership.

Once divided, one of the new counties was named after Sylvanus Phillips. At this time, Phillips had already acquired some 300 acres adjacent to the Mississippi River approximately 10 miles south of Sterling, which is believed to be the present-day site of Helena. He also owned land from Private Survey #2384, which has been called his homeplace. Records also display that Phillips had been granted some land, originally part of the Spanish Land Grants.

He aimed to attract settlers and grow Helena into an incorporated city. He partnered with William Russell, an experienced land speculator from St. Louis, whose lone interest was monetary gain. Russell had previously acquired land through the Spanish Land Grant by pledging allegiance to Spain, as did others. Phillips also saw an opportunity to make money, a bonus for his venture. So, he donated his land to the county to develop it into a city site. The two men then hired Nicholas Rightor, a US Government surveyor who platted the land into designated lots and streets. Once the land was platted, the United States government approved the claims awarded through the French and Spanish Land Grants. Rightor made Helena his home after he and Phillips formed a friendship. Rightor died in 1841.

On November 16, 1833, Helena was officially incorporated as a town named after Sylvanus Phillips' daughter, Helena Phillips. She died at age 15 on August 28, 1831, after a lengthy illness. Sylvanus did not live to see the town incorporated, as he passed away on October 31, 1830. However, on December 5, 1856, the General Assembly of Arkansas fully incorporated Helena as a city. This change defined the way Helena was governed. These changes required a mayor, city council members, and, of course, a tax collector, as well as clerks and other officials.

The last page of this chapter is the platted survey map of Helena in December 1820. It extends just beyond a partial block of Walker Street on the north and ends with Elm Street on the south. College Street is the last street to the west, with Water Street on the eastern section running parallel with the Mississippi River. This area is bounded by one square mile. Water Street and parts of Ohio Street no longer exist. The mighty Mississippi destroyed them during past floods.

It was apparent that the founders of Helena were very meticulous in how the proposed city was laid out to accommodate its future citizens. They provided an area for a Public Square surrounded by the corners of McDonough, Miller, Columbia, and Franklin streets.

The third Phillips County Court House was constructed in this location in 1869, but a tornado severely damaged it in 1886. Helena also suffered a severe fire that devastated several downtown businesses. As a result, raising enough funds to rebuild a new courthouse took a couple of decades. The old courthouse site was turned into the Solomon Playground, where I played many times as a youngster. The "new courthouse" is located at 622 Cherry Street, completed in 1914. In 1977, it was added to the National Register of Historic Places.

The plat of Helena consisted of 701 numbered lots, most of which were designated for private homes "for the purpose of promoting useful learning, and encouraging of settlement of useful and orderly citizens upon and in the neighborhood of their undivided lands." Notice two diagonal streets, McMicle and State, leading to the Public Square. These streets are no longer there. Were they fully developed before selling the lots? Phillips and Russell noted in their original Dedication Deed that there were undoubtedly lots dedicated to particular uses beneficial to the city for various needs. If the city or any organization did not build on these lots in a specific number of years, the lots would then be reopened for sale for private use.

Note the lots 660, 661, 662, 663, and 664. These lots ended on College Street at the end of McMicle Steet and were explicitly to be used "to build and erect thereon a college or good academy" within a twelve-year or less period. I suspect the name College Street was tied into the selection of its name. In 1949, my family moved to lot 647, directly across the street from the proposed college. It is at the end of Rightor Street, named after the surveyor Nicholas Rightor. Rightor was never completed as a thorough street connecting it to College Street. Lots on the proposed diagonal streets of McMicle and State were sold to individuals because they were never developed as planned.

To confirm Phillips and Russell were intent on making Helena a thriving city, see lots 569 and 570, along with 352 and 353. These lots were to be held for the construction "to build a church or house of prayer and public worship." Adjacent were lots 350 and 351 (not shown on this map) that were held for "the express condition a good School House is built thereon and used and occupied for that purpose within ten years."

Phillips and Russell also designed the streets and alleys with names fitting the particular landscape, person, tree, etc. One of the streets was even named Phillips. Lots 567 and 568 are drawn in the record book as a designated cemetery near the end of Creek Alley on the east side of York Street. I wonder if this cemetery was ever used because it is not named and displayed in the list of cemeteries. It is possible, though. As a kid, I remember that homes never occupied this lot.

This corner of Poplar and York was the number one hot spot where all the neighborhood kids hung out. It was located behind the Moore Hornor House, built in 1859 and converted into a hospital after the Civil War. Also, just a block southwest of this location was the Graveyard Hill Cemetery, privately owned by several people and used to inter their family and friends. The coffin that my friends found was in this area, where my story began.

Lot 13 was on the corner of Water and Porter Streets. It provided the owner the "exclusive right of keeping a Public Ferry from said Town across the Mississippi River shall forever belong to the Owners and Proprietor." They also provided, "The inhabitants of said Town shall at any time have the full and absolute right to raise, erect and build a levee around all that part of said Town lying between ... Mississippi River and the said properties." Of course, Helena suffered some severe flooding in the 1920s and 1930s before the levee was constructed. The parts of Water Street left after the flooding and erosion were covered over when the levee was built. The ferry moved to the end of Arkansas Street and remained there until the Helena Bridge was completed in 1961.

Sources:

Parts are copied with permission from *Reflections of the Past,*
Patricia Ann Smith, FB.
Phillips County Historical Quarterly VOL 1 No. 1, VOL 13 No. 2, VOL 15 #3, VOL 5 #4
Tri-County Genealogical Society VOL 3 No. 2
Arkansasheritage.com
Historical Sketch of the Hornor Family Since 1683
Almanac.com
Britannica Dictionary
Collins dictionary
hotsr.com Arkansas bears
history.cosl.org
Arkansas Democrat-Gazette, Arkansas Outdoors 4/21/2024, Bryan Hendricks

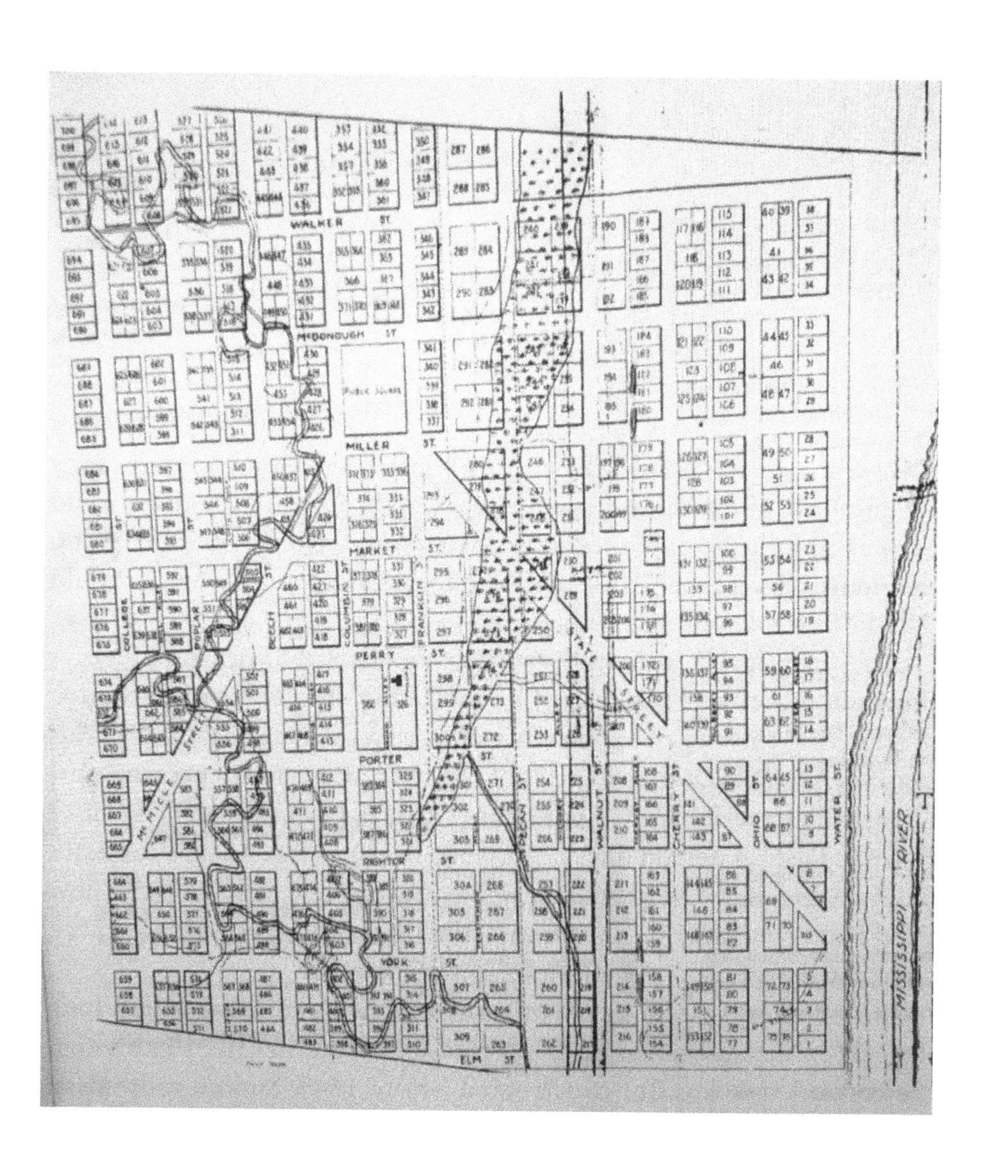

WALKER ST.
McDONOUGH ST
MILLER ST.
MARKET ST.
PERRY ST.
PORTER ST.
RIGHTOR ST.
YORK ST.
ELM ST.
COLLEGE
POPLAR
BEECH ST
COLUMBIA ST
FRANKLIN
WALNUT ST
STATE STREET
CHERRY ST
OHIO ST
WATER ST.
MISSISSIPPI RIVER

Chapter Seven

WHO WAS SHE?

So, who was the lady in the coffin? I have been asking myself many questions about this person for years, and suddenly, I realized I had been asking the wrong questions. My first question should be, "Who should this person be?" If I want to relocate and identify her, I should take a different approach.

As I mentioned earlier, it would be wonderful to proclaim everything about her life. She could be reburied in the center of Battery C overlooking the city of Helena. It would be a great addition to revealing Helena's past culture as part of the current revival featuring new historical attractions. We could honor this lady as a "Patron Saint of Helena's Past." A person does not have to be canonized to be a saint. It's like a phantasmagoric experience if I let my mind wander. We all know good people we refer to as saints. Other titles, such as sentinel, sentry, guardian, keeper, etc., may also be appropriate.

So far, in my searches, I have narrowed down a timeline of how long the lady in the coffin had been interred on Reservoir Hill. I know that the coffin I saw was not constructed before 1848, and no more dead were buried on the hill after 1865. I still don't have an exact timeline of when childhood friends found her. But, in talking with people I grew up with, I know it was between 1953 and 1959, and everyone agrees on this period.

A listing shows 75 bodies were moved from Graveyard Hill to Evergreen/Maple Hill Cemetery, all with passing dates before 1865. Only a few may have been left behind because the tombstones were destroyed on July 4, 1863, during the Battle of Helena. This lady's body was one and maybe the only one left in an iron coffin.

I wrote earlier that her coffin might have been dumped into the Mississippi River. However, through my investigation, I now discount this theory. That coffin was displayed in a restaurant in Memphis in 1958.

I have concluded that this coffin was moved to an undisclosed burial ground in or around Helena or relocated elsewhere on Reservoir Hill.

Wouldn't it be amazing to reveal the identity and circumstances of an unknown and forgotten person who was left behind 175 years ago? Wouldn't it be sensational to recall all of the stories we remember about Helena and share them with people visiting her new gravesite? And wouldn't it be remarkable if all of this was real? I mentioned earlier that I recalled she was wearing buckskins. What if she was clothed in a pink frilly dress, and it turned brown due to decomposition?

My dream of a future Patron Saint of Helena has deep roots in the grave of Adrienne Dumont atop Petit Jean Mountain near Morrilton, Arkansas. Adrienne was a young girl living in France in the early 1700s who was in love with a young French nobleman named Chavet. During this time, France explored the new world and claimed parts of the Louisiana Territory. I briefly touched on this in a previous chapter, explaining aspects of Phillips County belonging to the Empire of France and the Kingdom of Spain.

In 1803, the United States acquired all of this land by an agreement known as the Louisiana Purchase, which more than doubled its size. The historical ownership of this land is long and complicated. France, Spain, Great Britain, Haiti, and the Port of New Orleans played a part before the deal with the United States was finalized. There were many other factors, but too many to detail here. The 827,000 square miles cost $15 million, equating to just four cents an acre. Today's cost (2023) would represent $2.2 trillion, roughly between $1,480 and $4,420 per acre.

Chauvet had received permission from the King of France to travel and explore the land France had claimed. He was also in love with Adrienne, and they planned to be married. She wanted to wed immediately and accompany Chavet on his exploits, but he feared for her safety and thought they best marry upon his return. When he prepared to set sail from France, she dressed as a young boy, applied for, and received the position of cabin boy on the ship. Her disguise worked so well that no one discovered her identity until the ship sailed up the Arkansas River below the Mountain. Here, she became seriously ill and was forced to reveal her identity. She begged Chauvet for forgiveness, but the illness overtook her, and she died. Her disguise fooled everyone on the ship, earning the nickname Petit Jean, which means Little John in French. Today, her grave site is visible from the top of Petit Jean Mountain, near the edge overlooking the beautiful Arkansas River and its spectacular landscape.

I envision discovering the completely unknown information surrounding the lady in the coffin. Her remains were present on Graveyard/Reservoir Hill during the Civil War when her grave marker was destroyed. Most of the destruction of the tombstones was done by the *U.S.S. Tyler* gunboat firing all the 169 rounds of the Parrott artillery shells, each weighing 32 pounds. It was positioned on the Mississippi River just east of downtown Helena, a distance of less than a mile. The noise and another 264 rounds of 8-inch Dahlgren shells had to have been deafening and created horrible fears for the Confederate soldiers. The Union also fired from Battery D (Hindman Hill) on the south side, while some of its troops fired muskets from Fort Curtis below, both within a mile of Graveyard Hill. Because the Confederates felt confused and surrounded, they lost 500 to 600 soldiers by 12:30 p.m. History tells many of the wounded suffered in excruciating agony, expressing it with loud, painful cries. As a result, 1,200 Confederates laid down their rifles and surrendered.

The 75 or so bodies exhumed and moved to Evergreen Cemetery around 1870 were identified by whatever bits of markers remained and by loved ones knowing their locations. Her body was left undetected for nearly 90 years.

The legend of the *U.S.S. Tyler* is still a topic of conversation today. It had a previous life as a freight-passenger steamer. Being built in 1857 in

Cincinnati, Ohio, it was named the *A.O. Tyler.* In 1861, she was converted to a gunboat with a new name and ordered to join the United States Navy.

The owner of the freight-passenger steamer was a Southerner named Samuel Rodgers. Sympathizing with the South, he appealed to the Secretary of War to change the name to A.O. Taylor. The Secretary agreed, but the story says there was confusion with the spelling, so most people referred to it as the *U.S.S. Tyler.*

Once refitted, she was 180 feet long, 42 feet wide, and weighed approximately 535 tons. Powered by three boilers fueled by coal, her speed averaged between 7 and 10 knots. She was armed with one 32-pounder Parrott cannon and six 8-inch Dahlgren's firing a 24-pound shell. Like most naval stories

from the Civil War, she was not an ironclad vessel. Her defense depended on luck and the five-inch-thick oak bulwarks protecting the upper deck and pilot house.

The *Tyler* spent time on the Mississippi River at the mouth of the White River and patrolled along the Yazoo River. On June 15, 1862, while on the Yazoo, she came under attack by *CSS Arkansas,* a rebel ironclad, and suffered damage, but managed to escape and continued to engage in other battles. Logs also say it took a couple of days before the Battle of Helena to have her boilers repaired in Memphis and coaled (loaded with coal to be used for fuel). At 7:30 a.m. on July 4, 1863, the day of the Battle of Helena, she opened fire, unleashing her might on the Confederates on Graveyard Hill.

Before her presence in the Battle of Helena on July 4, 1863, *U.S.S. Tyler* had participated in the Vicksburg Campaign in 1862 for approximately a month. She assisted in an organized operation involving land troops and water attacks.

Vicksburg finally fell on July 4, 1863, the same day the Union fought and won the Battles of Helena and Gettysburg. This day gave the Union complete control of the Mississippi River's navigational system and severely hampered the Confederacy in receiving military supplies.

The following is an unedited letter from the archive of an Iowa Soldier who fought during the Civil War, Private Newton Robert Scott,

Company A, of the 36th Infantry, Iowa Volunteers. This letter was sent to his parents, Hullum and Mary Scott of Albia, Monroe County, Iowa, written in his own words with his original spelling, just two days after the Battle of Helena. It details and describes what took place during and after the Battle.

Helena Arks
July 6th 1863

Dear Parents

I will Inform with Pleasure that I am well at the Present & I Hope that when this Reaches you that it May find you all well I Had a light chill yesterday But I feel all O.K. to day

Ere this time I suppose you Have the News of the Battle at Helena I will tell you that Gens Price Holmes and Marmaduke made a Dash at us on the Morning of the 4th. Inst 5 Brigades of Infty & Considerably Cavalry When I a wake up the long Roll was Sounding & Every things to arms The Pickets was fighting and By Daylight our Forces Were all in Positions our artillery all Ready & the Drove our Pickets in to the Rifle Pits where our men were & the Fight was Most Sanguine & the massed there Force one the Center & that confined the Fighting on the Bluffs all this time our Hill Batterys ten or twelve Pieces in the Bottom & the Gun Boat Tyler with 8 or ten guns were throwing Shells Amongst them thick as Hail But they Filled up there Fallen ranks with Fresh Troops & about 8 oclock they made a Charge on one of our Batterys first on the Rifle Pits they Carried the Rifle P bits & Come a head on the Battery & took the Battery the Rebels was

now in Fare view & our Artillery just mowed them & our Infty Had a Cross fire on them & they could not Stand it & Part of the run for life But the most of them Surrendered I See them Coming over our Rifle Pits & take our Battery But they had not to Spike the cannons for the Shells & Bullets were to Hot for them

We took 960 Prisners with 3 Cols & 3 or 4 other Field Oficers & Sent them up the River in 2 Hours after they were taken We Have Over 400 of there wounded Here in town I talked with Several of there wounded & they Said that Gen Holmes was Killed he was Chief Commander & Price next & then Marmeduke the 2nd. Arks was on the Extreme left Supporting a Battery our Battery Done great Execution

We was not in Gun Shot of them But could See them Fighting all the time & there Balls whistled all around us & Amongst us one Ball wounded 2 Darkies in the Arm not Dangerous

I Have no time to give you any Detail now But will as Soon as I can

I was Over apart of the Battle Field yesterday & Indeed it was a Awful Sight where the charged on one of our Batterys I Stood & Counted 35 Dead Rebels in about 20 Paces Square But not Being verry well I did not go over But a Small Space on the Battle ground & I counted 78 Dead Rebels & what little Space I was Over we Had Details out yesterday all Day burying there Dead an Officer Come to me this morning for a nother Detail to Bury more Dead today He Said that that they Had Burried about 400 of there Dead

all Ready from Best Accounts they have lost in Killed wounded & Prisoners about 2000 & on Our Side we have lost in Killed wounded not Over one Hundred & we lost 4 or 5 Prisners of our Pickets

You will think that unresponsible to tell Such a one sided fight But wait for Official Reports the 36th. Iowa was on the Extreme right & lost 3 Prisners & one Killed on Picket. Co A lost none we Recd news this morning By 2 Boats that Vicksburg Surrendered on the 4th. At ten Oclock Hurrah for Such Celebrations as at Vicksburg & Helena on 4th. July 1863 we can whip ten to one of the Rebels.

Here now you can See what we can Do Behind our works

I will write again as soon as I can & tell you all Huzza for the Old Flag of our Union

We Had one gunboat Here in the fight & now we Have 3 good ones So let them Come

I am sorrow to Inform you that Will Holmes is verry Sick in Hospital I see Him 2 days ago & not Heard from Him since, Case Critical Have Bin the Rifle Pits for the last 48 Hours Capt Elder & 2nd. Lieut are not Able for Duty Which throw all tasks on me & 1st. Leiut

I have no room for my Name But I will Scribble Down Here Old Dempsey Newton Scott

The present-day archives of the dead, wounded, and missing differ considerably from the letter written by Private Newton Scott. Historyofwar.org lists Confederates as 173 dead, 687 wounded, and 776 missing or captured. En.wikipedia.org lists Confederates as 169 dead, 659 wounded, and 786 wounded or missing. Other reports claim varying numbers. I can understand a young man possibly being in shock a couple of days after a bloody battle. Also, the reporting back then was done by word of mouth as there were no sophisticated electronic tools for recording. He did say he counted 113 Confederate dead. The 960 prisoners and the burial of 400 are a bit of a stretch compared to the transcripts we have today. I do, however, wonder if all of the bodies of dead Confederate soldiers buried on the battlefield were eventually moved to the Confederate Cemetery or other places.

It's logical to have buried the dead as quickly as possible, but I wonder who buried them. Private Newton Scott indicates in his letter that the Union soldiers did this, but I think that was highly unlikely if they had taken so many Confederate prisoners. The spoils of war do have advantages! In this case, I feel the Confederates had the gruesome task of taking care of their dead under the supervision of the Union. If the Union did bury the Confederates, it was probably done in a common grave.

Private Newton Robert Scott, Company A, of the 36th Iowa Infantry, fought in the Battle of Helena; Minos Miller, an African American, participated in the battle, too. Miller was 21 years old and also belonged to the 36th Iowa Infantry, but in Company D. His Negro unit was present when the Confederates attacked, occupying the far-left side of the Union line. The issuance of the Emancipation Proclamation allowed Negros to serve. Still, because they had yet to reach the required number of troops, the unit was not officially mustered into federal service. His regiment spent its time drilling and organizing. In December 1863, Miller accepted a promotion to second lieutenant with Company F, 54th Colored Infantry. He wrote many letters to his mother, which provided a detailed collection of historical insight into the Civil War while serving as an African-American. These letters are stored at the University of Arkansas in Fayetteville.

1869, the Phillips County Memorial Association was formed to begin organizing and moving the Confederate dead to a single location where they could be honored. The upper west side of Evergreen Cemetery was the perfect spot for the newly designated Confederate Cemetery. The Association purchased this one-acre site for $1.

Around 300 Confederate soldiers were buried there, including those who died in the Battle of Helena, others from different battles, and those who passed later due to wounds. Also, soldiers living in Phillips County who had survived the war became eligible to be interred in the cemetery when they died. Most of the dead were accounted for, and their graves were marked when moved to the cemetery. However, some were unknown, and their stones are marked as such. Although some Union soldiers fell, they were not buried with the Confederate dead. At least three bodies of Union soldiers found were later transported to Memphis and Louisville for burial.

As kids, we played all over these hills; the only body found was the lady in the coffin. Of course, none of the soldiers would have been buried in coffins back then due to the speed of the interment process when cleaning up the battlefield. The location on Graveyard Hill, where the coffin was found, versus the site of the soldiers' burials and the pre-Civil War burials, gives me hope that this was the only one overlooked.

Sources:

Arkansasstateparks.com
Phillips County Historical Society Publication VOL 3 # 1, VOL 15 # 2, VOL 35 #1 & 2
Nationalgeographic.com
En.m.wikipedia.org
Historyofwar.org
teachingamericanhistory.org, protesting the Louisiana Purchase
wikimedia.org/wikipedia/commons/3/30/USS Tyler 1857.jpg
civilwarvirtualmuseum.org/186-1862/african-americans-in-the-war/minos-miller-letters.php

Chapter Eight

WATER, WATER, EVERYWHERE—NUMBER, PLEASE

Graveyard Hill was not a formal cemetery but was frequently called "City Cemetery." Different individuals and families privately owned sections of it for their use but periodically granted permission for burial to friends. The bombardment during the Civil War destroyed grave markers, making it impossible to recover lost graves some years later. The hill was composed of plain brown loam, which washed away during heavy rains because no kudzu was growing. Kudzu was introduced in the 1930s, and most trees were removed as part of the battleground tactics. Most of them have not regrown.

The city of Helena formally purchased land for a cemetery and started moving bodies in 1870. Little evidence was kept or needed to be completed because it was sketchy. The bodies found without markers were moved from the hill and buried in an area of Evergreen Cemetery designated for paupers. Many opinions are still open about where the paupers are laid to rest. Even though the Maple Hill Cemetery Company and the city leaders agreed in 1899 to provide a space for newly washed-up bodies, specific records still need to be found. So, attaching names to unknown bodies and not knowing where they were reinterred has left them forever lost. An example was published in the *Helena Weekly Clarion* of December 8, 1869, stating, "All persons having relatives interred in the

Cemetery lately laid out by the undersigned will please come forward and point out the place and, if necessary, have the remains removed. All those not removed or otherwise provided for by the 1st day of January, next, will be removed to that part of the Cemetery appropriated to the Potter Field."

Helena, located on the banks of the Mississippi, along with the nearby St. Francis River just north of town and numerous other bodies of water, had ample water supply. Of course, this supply did not mean the water was safe for consumption during the city's early history. There was no central city waterworks. Most people relied on cisterns for their water. The early half of the 1800s describes several little townships surrounding the area as being in the river bottom using principally water from the Mississippi or from shallow wells they dug because the water was plentiful. Others trapped it in rain barrels and devised their storage systems. Any water used for cooking or washing had to be brought into the house by buckets. Some stories tell how the drinking water was kept in cedar buckets with a nearby dipper shared by all.

Most of these areas were frequently flooded, causing the water supply to become contaminated, resulting in sickness and diseases. Because of so much water and unsanitary conditions, the lowlands were a breeding ground for mosquitoes carrying yellow fever bacteria. Cholera and scarlet fever also increased mortality, and yellow fever took many lives during the mid-1850s. Other sicknesses, such as dysentery and typhoid fever, also added to the discomfort of the citizens. The construction of the levees began in 1897 and extended coverage in 1907, 1914, and 1927.

During these times, the citizens of Helena realized they needed to protect the water supply from disease and create more measures to curtail flooding. The Helena Improvement District was organized to address these issues. Plans were laid out to extend the levee from Walker Street to Hanks Lane on the south side of town. Most of Walker Street, extending west to Beach Street, had already been elevated into a levee separating it from downtown Helena.

The elevation of Walker Street was not just dirt. An extensive covered drainage system was built with reinforced concrete and connected to other culverts. This construction reduced the overflow of water to the downtown section by fifty percent. The area north of Walker Street became known as North Helena, and Walker Street was generally nicknamed Walker Levee. The west end of Walker at Beech Street is connected to higher ground and is part of Crowley's Ridge. There was no chance of the river ever flooding this area. For the most part, the levees reduced flooding and the possibility of contamination.

The Helena Waterworks was established in 1892-1893 but only provided water for personal use. The sewer system was added in 1902-1903. However, these improvements did not eliminate the possibility of contamination as the mighty river still posed flooding by infiltrating the systems.

After years of searching and experimenting for artesian well water, Nicholas Straub found it on his property. Straub Lane in Helena is named after him and is located east of Biscoe, just across the street from Estevan Hall. By 1891, Helena had discovered that water could be delivered from the artesian wells below the earth. The analysis determined that wells should be drilled and water pumped to a high point for delivery as height also pressurizes the system. Graveyard Hill was the highest point and fit that need.

By this time, everyone thought all of the graves had been moved and subsequently began to refer to the hill as Reservoir Hill because this is where the city had planned to build a water reservoir. I'm sure that during this era, after many years, most people forgot that the hill was once a cemetery. Anyone who remembered probably wanted to forget that their water was coming from where the dead were once buried.

The city began to search for a way to finance the reservoir and found a wealthy retired lawyer and investor named Judge Robert M. Foster from St. Louis. In 1895, he provided the funds required for a pumping and drilling station located on Saint Francis Street and the reservoir on the hill by securing a mortgage of $60,000. The judicial sale on March 26, 1895, describes how "the pump house, boilers, pumps and machinery of every character and description and property together with the reservoir, pipes and connections thereon all the mains, services, connection, meters, hydrants, rights of way, franchises, easements, tools, implements, office fixtures and furniture be given over to Robert M. Foster." After this agreement, The Helena Water Company belonged to one man.

I assume this is the demarcation point in Helena's history, where the name "Hill" was forever changed from Graveyard to Reservoir. My parents were born in the second decade of the 1900s and never referred to the hill by any name other than Reservoir Hill. As kids, it was the only name we knew. My grandfather, Sam Saia, only spoke of St. Mary's, the Catholic cemetery. He was born in 1883 and moved to Helena in 1910.

If you travel to Helena today and ask current residents about Graveyard Hill, they are perplexed. Recently, I spoke with Al Haraway, a 93-year-old gentleman who had lived in or near Helena for most of his life. He told me he had only recently learned Reservoir Hill was formerly a cemetery. Not knowing about the former name must have made the water taste better!

By 1899, Maple Hill Cemetery was going through several cosmetic changes as well as structural updates. No one thought about Graveyard Hill any longer. The three or four avenues running through the cemetery had been graded and paved with fresh gravel. There was enough room for pedestrians to stroll between the graves while admiring the newly trimmed shrubs and attractively pruned trees. Hunting on the cemetery grounds was forbidden. Children had to be accompanied by their parents, and no dogs were allowed within 100 yards of the boundary. The beautiful new landscape was an enviable sight for other cemeteries across the state. This stunning new city of the dead even had a keeper's lodge with water connected to the Walker Street mains, which received pure water from atop Reservoir Hill. The cycle of life seemed to follow the deceased citizens!

Now, after more than 160 years, this beautiful resting place shows its age. Plans are being made to establish a million-dollar endowment fund to return Maple Hill to its graceful past. This information is posted on its *Facebook page.*

"Since 1861, Maple Hill Cemetery has kept the remains and memories of thousands of Helena's residents, but now, with few burials and a declining population, the future upkeep of Maple Hill is uncertain. Therefore, we are raising an endowment to guarantee its upkeep for generations, preserving our history, and maintaining the remains and memory of our departed for generations to come."

The living residents also wanted to get in on the new modern technology before taking permanent residence in Maple Hill. The cemetery board called for installing one of those new talking machines, better known as a telephone. It was installed inside the "commodious keepers lodge, accommodating the lot owners and the management."Having a telephone in those days came with complications. Some citizens began to refer to the phone as a "common nuisance." Some complaints said the operators were poorly trained and could not correctly connect callers. Others said they were underpaid because of the numerous calls. Others were being connected to wrong numbers, causing frustration due to the babble of different voices traveling over the lines simultaneously. One of the biggest concerns was that people had lost their privacy. Anyone could hear your conversation by simply ringing in and listening. Some complained that after hanging up, they would try to "ring up" later and notice they were still connected. People didn't refer to your telephone "number" but to your telephone "connection." Numbers were given out in the order in which they were purchased. For example, if you owned the first phone in a city, your number was 1. It was common for neighbors to have numbers like 13, 17, 21, etc.   There were, however, some good things that came from the telephone. See this little blurb in The *Forrest City Times* on September 1, 1899.

Miss May Toomer, a charming young lady of Helena, passed through the city Sunday en route home from a visit to home folks in Chicago and on the Great Lakes. We met the young lady through the kindness of Mrs. Prude, and found that she was an operator at the telephone exchange in Helena. She was real pleasant and pretty too, for that matter.

Not only did the telephone open up a new means of communication, but it also provided opportunities for unlimited income and new jobs. Within a couple of years, people could make calls across the state and the nation with connections linking callers to one another.

TO MAKE BIG MONEY selling our Electric Telephone. Best seller on earth. Sent all complete ready to set up; lines of any distance. A practical Electric Telephone. Our agents making $5 to $10 a day easy. Everybody buys; Big money without work. Prices low. Any one can make $75 per month. Address W. P. Harrison & Co., Clerk No. 11, Columbus, Ohio.

shortening labor.

Miss Edna Williams, the efficient manager of the Telephone Exchange in this city for the past several years, has been transferred to the Little Rock office, where she will have less work and responsibility, but where she will be advanced to a higher position in the company's service. When Miss Williams took charge of the Helena Exchange there were 80 subscribers; now there are 245. During the years when this growth was attained Miss Williams was the careful, conscientious, indefatigable, faithful manager, discharging her whole duty to employers and patrons alike. She has earned her promotion by hard, faithful work. The World, with her many friends in this city, wishes for her continued prosperity and numerous promotions.

The World acknowledges the receipt

The pumping station secured its water from four wells that were more than 500 feet deep and powered by two Worthington Duplex pumps. They pumped 2,000,000 gallons per day for a total of 4,000,000 gallons. The water was sent up to the newly built cement reservoir atop Reservoir

Hill, which just happened to have a storage capacity of 4,000,000 gallons. The container was completed in 1892. It was 196 feet long, 66 feet wide, 16 feet deep, and had a cement cover. By 1899, improvements were already being made to ensure the supply of pure water by reinforcing the top, making it inaccessible to any animal or plant life. The only entrance was through a trap door with stairs, making it handy for cleaning when necessary. The door was securely locked to assure customers that no foreign materials could contaminate the water.

The height of the reservoir on the hill allowed gravity to work its magic by distributing the water at 60 pounds of pressure for general use and 120 pounds to its 151 fire hydrants across the city. In September 1892, the city council tested this pressure with many citizens on hand as witnesses. A hose with a diameter of 2½ inches and 190 feet long successfully threw a stream of water 90 feet high through a one-inch nozzle. A further test threw a 60-foot-high stream through a 350-foot hose.

Because the reservoir was high on the hill, this provided the necessary gravitational pressure to push the needed water down to the people of Helena. However, unforeseen problems did occur in 1899 when a crack developed in the bottom of the cement floor, and all the water escaped. The weight of the cement top may have caused the problem. Water shortages caused several large lumber mills in the south part of town to shut down. The Helena Compress Company continued to operate but at a slower pace. The pumps continued to run and supply enough water for the average consumer, but they were asked to refrain from sprinkling the unpaved dusty streets and their lawns until the repairs were complete. The following year, in 1900, soil was washed away on the reservoir's northeast side, resulting in a landslide that badly damaged the walls and caused more leakage. These problems were solved by constructing another wall supported with brick terracing and cement.

By 1910, Judge Foster was ready to transfer ownership of the waterworks company to the city of Helena as required by the city's charter. The First National Bank of Helena selected a special arbitrator to negotiate the right of purchase. After being appraised, according to the charter requirements, the city gave notice, and the waterworks officially became the Helena Water Company.

In 1911, the City of Helena reported one of the state's lowest mortality rates because there were only 22 deaths in the last half of the year. It was reported that only a few had been infectious.

Cisterns were a thing of the past. By this time, water was even being supplied to the newly growing town of West Helena. Helena was starting to move into the 20th century and began to pass ordinances requiring clean water delivery. During the January city hall meeting of 1910, the council demanded that the Helena Water Company be required to furnish pure water under the terms of the agreement. The council passed a law to fine the water company $25 per day if it was determined that the water was impure. In addition to the clean water, Helena made other remarkable advances in early 1911 when the citizens decided to have all the streets paved. A big push was put on to get this done when a slogan was created, and people started wearing buttons reading "Get Out of the Mud."

Improvements continued, and in 1959, *Helena World* reported that the "Helena water supply has again met the United States Public Health Service bacteriological quality standard." This approval was the result of the new $130,000 water filtration plant.

Sources:

Patricia Ann Smith, FB October 28, 2021
Helena Weekly Clarion, December 8, 1869
Phillips County Historical Quarterly Vol 11 No. 3
The *Helena Weekly World,* 1915, March 1, 1899, April 12, 1899, October 11, 1899
The Monticellonian April 5,1892-June 22, 1911; The *Osceola Times* April 30, 1892 - Newspapers.com
Daily Arkansas Gazette January 5, 1911
The *Helena World,* January 10, 1910, August 16, 1899, March 9, 1895, December 31, 1902, May 10, 1899

Phillips County Historical Society Spring Issue December 1982-March 1983
The Southern Standard April 5, 1895
The *Forrest City Times* September 1, 1899, April 28, 1899
Helena World, 1959-Helena Water System receives state approval

Chapter Nine

GET OUT OF THE MUD

As the 19th century drew to a close and the 20th began, Helena kept pace and started to improve its streets and roads leading to and from the city. In the early few years of the 1900s, most streets were dirt. Citizens owning lots, initially platted in 1820 when the first map was drawn up, were required to provide sidewalks along the streets. The dirt streets were sprinkled with water by people who owned homes to keep the dust down when they became scorched and dusty. When it rained, they became intolerable. I can't imagine people entering their homes with their shoes covered in mud.

Since most transportation at this time was non-mechanical, the only roads were dirt streets. Naturally, citizens picked up mud and muck from walking around the neighborhood. As a result, the city officials passed Ordinance No. 1189 in 1902. It required property owners to have "lots abutting the streets of Helena to build and maintain suitable sidewalks." There were specific requirements as to size and the material used in construction. Only oak, pine, or cypress wood less than two inches thick could be used, and the planks had to be laid out lengthwise. The walks also had to be adequately supported. The ordinance also stated that if anyone wanted to use something other than wood, such as brick, stone, or concrete, it could be substituted as long as it was laid out properly and satisfactorily.

Streets were to be paved with vitrified bricks, becoming popular nationwide. It was apparent Cherry Street had become the main street in Helena as early as April of 1903 when the city council unanimously passed an ordinance providing funds for its paving. Members were very confident and excited that the streets of Helena "would be in better shape than they had ever been before." But, like today, projects take time and money to materialize. It was in October 1905 when the actual paving started. A sub-drain had to be constructed, and a foundation of gravel and concrete was laid on a cinder bed. Cherry Street property owners had to sign a contract to pay a stipulated amount for the street improvement in front of their premises. The city had already approved $6,500 for the paving of the intersections.

The earliest big boom for Cherry Street came between 1910 through 1919 when it consisted of nearly 20 saloons. Many other stores and establishments also made it a popular location. On Saturday nights, businesses were open until midnight because workers from the levee and timber camps poured into town. Some arrived on barges, and others came from the new streetcar line. Cherry Street was so crowded that it was difficult to stroll along even at midnight.

As years passed, the levee was completed. The mechanization of farm equipment eliminated jobs, and the forestry industry slowed down. In 1934, the streetcar line closed, and the economy slowed down. But Cherry Street survived and was back in business by the 1950s. I remember those years very well. I worked at C.E. Mayer's department store throughout high school. We were open until 9 p.m. every Saturday. There were no saloons, only a few scattered "honky-tonks" on other nearby streets. The kids were making the drag, and many people were shopping. Mexican farm laborers filled the streets, and the restaurants were busy.

Cherry Street and Helena may be going through some hard times today, but I'm convinced it will return. Significant strides have already been made with the annual King Biscuit Blues and Delta Dirt Blues Festivals. Helena is taking advantage of its history and building parks and informative historical attractions.

Several of the original brick-paved streets in Helena are still in use and visible today. Back then, vitrified bricks were made through annealing, making them more durable than conventional bricks. Being fired at higher temperatures and for extended periods made them water-resistant and more reliable. Although some roadway areas are wavy, the bricks still perform their job. I would have loved to have seen the original paved brick streets. I bet they were beautiful! The last 300 feet on the east end of Elm Street is a prime example of the sustainability of the brick. It is in excellent shape and looks like it was just recently constructed.

Over the years, I have heard some people refer to the streets as cobblestone. After researching, I found cobblestone had been used for hundreds of years and was initially dubbed in England in the 1400s and 1500s. Although it is as hard as vitrified brick, it is a naturally rounded stone and better suited for building construction. Vitrified brick is shaped to fit together and provide a flat surface for wheels to roll smoothly.

As time progressed, more and more people wanted Helena to join the "paving boom" and have their streets upgraded. In 1905, Mr. J.B. Pillow offered to pay for one-half of the cost of paving his street if the city would agree to foot the bill for the remainder of the work. The city council approved his offer and put up $650 to complete the deal as long as the work was done under the supervision of the city engineer. This move opened the door for more residential areas to follow suit when the city council resolved to provide two-thirds of future expenses on paving. Citizens began to form neighborhood districts to advance the paving of streets further. A five-block area on the north end of town was already under contract with vitrified brick. This area was part of Columbia Street and some of the McDonough and Miller Streets regions. Beech Street was bricked in 1912 for a cost of $27,000. Most of this part of the original bricking has remained intact for some 100-plus years. Only a few sections are slightly wavy due to soil movement.

In 1912, Helena was praised for being one of the "best-paved communities in the state" thanks to a combination of individual property owners and city contracts. By 1913, an agreement was granted to allow Columbia Street to be wholly bricked while Walnut Street had just been finished.

In 1919, the citizens of West Helena had successfully persuaded the council to pave some of the streets with concrete. Later in the year,

Helena made provisions to acquire $550,000 to pave seven miles of city streets with the pavement.

West Helena was missing from the map in the 1910 census and only had a population of 1,500. The paving of Perry and Poplar Streets laid the groundwork for a pathway between cities, with a mile of the streetcar line being completed. By May 1912, the streetcar line opened between the two towns, powered with electricity furnished by the new electric plant on Hanks Lane. The new plant had a capacity of around 100,000 kilowatts. The streetcar line's rolling stock included three trailers. Three open and three closed vehicles cost just five cents for travel.

At this time, Helena was referred to as aristocratic, and West Helena as energetic and progressive. Helena had been known as a cotton hub for years, and the timber industry also grew to help fuel the local economy. West Helena became home to a new Country Club, which attracted the Press Association and just happened to be located on the new highway between the two cities. As the two towns expanded, The Helen and West Helena Street Railway claimed to own 16 passenger-carrying cars. The postmaster even considered placing boxes for mail collection on the vehicles.

By 1920, parts of Phillips County around Helena had 125 miles of concrete roadways laid out in all directions, and the city undertook improvements in drainage canals serving business and residential areas. Solid cement routes to Marvell and Old Town were also underway. Highway travel was becoming a way of life, and weather reporting became a new tool for motorists. The *Arkansas Democrat* began to feature reports on those dirt roads unsuitable for driving by describing the intensity of projected amounts of rain and warning of slippery, muddy places.

Meanwhile, road and street building were improving. Proper grading, guttering, curbing, and paving were installed on new projects. Brick streets were becoming a thing of the past with the development of asphalt, concrete, tarvia, creosoted wooden blocks, and bitumen. As early as 1918, asphalt became a favorite road paver because it was easy to mend. Repairs could be made in short order with a barrel of hot asphalt, a shovel, a wheelbarrow, and a few five-eighth-inch rocks.

Sidewalks were being constructed with better, longer-lasting materials and becoming a necessary part of the landscape in wealthier neighborhoods. The streets around the Catholic school even had sufficient funds to build four blocks of new concrete sidewalks. As a kid, I remember some of these older sections where tree roots had grown so large they pushed up the walks. Trees were planted as part of the landscape shortly after the sidewalks were constructed a half-century earlier, and many are still living today.

The material used in making the streets revealed a lot about a neighborhood—the width and height of the curbs provided information about who lived there. The poorer areas had open ditches, while the wealthier sections had underground guttering.

Because Helena had developed a system of tax districts, some citizens paid for part of the street paving, and people in these areas were better off than those in other parts of the city. For example, North Helena had very few streets with curbs. Most of those streets were the last paved, and many were paved with cinder. In 1912, Helena was divided into ten districts and was rated as a distinguished municipality in Arkansas because of the amount of paving. Because of this, some citizens suggested to the city council that the entire corporate limits fall under one district and that the entire city be paved. Property owners rapidly defeated this idea because they felt their areas would be better served with separate sections rather than just one city-wide district.

I grew up on Holly Street in North Helena. It was paved with cinder. I mentioned earlier that brick and concrete streets were laid over a cinder bed. Because North Helena was a poorer section, the cinder-bedded streets were as good as it got. The residents felt blessed to have some ground cover to help keep the dust down and the muddy road somewhat overcoated.

Despite Holly Street running through the poorer part of Helena, it had a special significance! At one time or another, almost every citizen who traveled from one end to the other to either St. Mary's Catholic Cemetery, Temple Beh El Cemetery, or Maple Hill Cemetery could only reach them by traveling on Holly Street. Citizens either traveled behind a funeral procession when they could or were later transported in a hearse!

Cinder is an aggregate coarse-to-medium particulate material consisting of sand, gravel, crushed stone, slag, or leftover concrete and asphalts. Over time, the cinder got stronger because it was frequently re-cindered and covered with smelly, thick tar or oil. This combination caused the materials to meld together and provide a hard surface. There were no gutters, curbs, or sidewalks, only open ditches on both sides of the road—culverts connected under the intersections. Kids could play in the ditches and crawl through the culverts to the other side of the street. The city mainly depended on the earth to absorb the water runoff. This policy and the closeness to the river are why Helena had such a rich supply of artesian well water.

Being such an aristocratic city with a streetcar line, Helena realtors began advertising some houses with access. For example, one ad read, "Choice 6-room bungalow, on car line and paved street; modern in every way; only $1,400; on terms, PEYTON JOHNSON Jr., with Polk Real Estate Co., phone 1917." The car line also allowed people to travel more easily to and from jobs.

Shades of racism existed then, which would not be permissible today. This ad posted reflects the issue. "WANTED- A refined white girl to do upstairs work and assist in the care of two children, ages 6 and 3 years; references required. Address MRS. SEELEG L. MUNDT, 1198 Perry St., Helena, Ark."

Another reads, "Middle-aged white woman to do general housework and care for an elderly lady; want a person that is in good health, reliable and unincumbered and able to do all work; only one in family; salary $15 per month; permanent position to right party. Apply to MRS. A COT-TEM, Box 586, Helena, Ark." I think the "unincumbered" is essential here because it sounds like the elderly lady required her assistant not to be personally involved with anyone else.

Unincumbered was important in this ad, as was WHITE. "A WHITE, unincumbered, experienced housemaid, for general housework; good home and wages to the right party. Write at once, with references, to MRS.ED WEIL. 727 Franklin Street, Helena, Ark."

Race played a part in other jobs as well. "WANTED—100-colored laborers for steam shovel, track laying, etc., at Helena Ark; one year's work, $1.75 per day. Apply on the job, THOMAS-HANNON CO., contractors and engineers, Helena, Ark."

In the 1940s and 1950s, the color of one's skin was important to a lot of people in the South. Public water fountains were posted with signs reading "White" or "Colored." If people of color were caught drinking from a fountain marked White, they were severely chastised. Today, restrooms are not designated for color but only for "men" or "women." Some are trending toward "occupied" or" vacant." I've even seen signs reading, "WHATEVER, just please wash your hands."

Sources:

Newspapers.com
The *Helena Weekly World* September 3, 1902, August 29, 1910
Daily Arkansas Gazette April 25, 1903, October 3, 1905; June 17, 1913; July 2, 1919; December 3, 1912; June 29, 1918; November 23, 1912; July 7, 1912; July 3, 1913; November 11, 1913, November 1, 1910
Mindat.org
Historicpavement.com
Arkansas Democrat July 9, 1905, December 13, 1920, October 16, 1912
Pine Bluff Daily Graphic June 11, 1920
The *Cambridge Tribune*, Volume 39, No. 29, September 16, 1916
The *Log Cabin Democrat* June 22, 1920
ECOBEAR Biohazard cleaning company
The *Osceola Times* March 29, 1918
Phillips County Historical Review Vol 27 No 1
Gone to the Grave by Abby Burnett
Wikipedia, Construction aggregate

Chapter Ten

THE FORGOTTEN GENERAL

Location on the banks of the Mississippi River in the nineteenth and for part of the twentieth century was advantageous for the city of Helena. The fact that the Battle of Helena even took place proves this point. Several other towns, cities, and locations across the South did not draw the attention of the Union. Helena was a logistical base for Vicksburg and Little Rock. In some ways, Helena's access to the Mississippi River gave it the equivalence of a larger city, such as Memphis or New Orleans. It was an essential hub for gathering Delta-raised cotton being exported to England. The Confederate losses of the Battles of Helena, Vicksburg, and Gettysburg on July 4, 1863, was a significant turning point in the Civil War, cutting off needed funds to continue the war.

After the war, Helena resumed as an important port city for river traffic. The automobile had yet to be invented, but the rail system was growing. Although steamships exported mainly cotton and lumber, they also transported everything else, earning them the nickname of packet boats. A packet boat usually traveled on a fixed route carrying anything from mail to goods and passengers, and frequently at the same time. Helena's location through the river was significantly important for the cotton and lumber industries.

As the railroads developed through the 1880s and the twentieth century emerged, more tracks were laid across the country. The lumber cut from the forests provided the necessary ties used by the railroad to spread its' tracks. It took about 2,200 railroad ties to support one mile of rail. Helena had access as a member of the Iron Mountain Railroad connected to the main line at Knobel, Arkansas, in Clay County. This connection provided Phillips County entry to all points across the entire country. Because of the railroads, the freight river traffic slowed for Helena, and most lumber products began to be shipped by rail. Cotton had also become "king" during this time, so compress companies laid rails right next to their docks, eliminating the need to transport bales waiting for boats on the river.

Although the method of shipping lumber and cotton had been diverted to rail transportation as time passed, the steamboats still found ways to be profitable. They began to move a variety of products as well as passengers. Some boats even became noted as places where people could frolic and gamble. Thus, the term "riverboat gambler" emerged and was attached to those patrons who lived on the boats and were employed to handle the cargo while in ports. Between ports, they gambled. In some ways, this resembled the life of a sharecropper on water because their pay remained on board.

As more passengers traveled along the rivers, the steamboats upgraded the cabins and services. The so-called riverboat gamblers became cabin boys, baggage handlers, and, intermittently, deckhands. The steamboats were not limited to the Mississippi River but utilized its tributaries connecting cities such as Cincinnati, Pittsburgh, Saint Louis, and beyond.

More steamboat lines opened for business. Some concentrated on transporting various types of freight, such as food products and household items, while others hauled livestock or whatever needed to be shipped. All of them allowed room for passengers. At one time, there were 56 landings along the Mississippi between Memphis and Helena.

The *Kate Adams* became a prominent passenger favorite, running a consistent schedule between Memphis and Helena. It offered luxurious cabins finished in beautiful cherry, mahogany, and maple hardwoods. There were also windows and electric lights. Delicious meals and drinks were served in the saloon, and passengers could dance and play various games of chance. Of course, there was always time to spend on the deck admiring the scenery. It must have felt like a river cruise on the Danube!

The sound of its whistle could identify each steamboat. People who lived along the river knew the particular sound of each boat and recognized it immediately. The Lee Lines' whistles were faint compared to the deep bullfrog sound of the *Kate Adams*. Radar and modern-day technology were unavailable during this era, so the whistle served many purposes. It announced the boats' approach to the landing or when traveling through foggy, dark, or curvy areas, warning other steamboats of its presence. It was a unique form of communication for river travel. It also served the pilot very well from his pilot house when giving various orders to his steam engineers while they worked in other areas on the boat.

In 1852, Congress passed a law regulating river navigation, which became a universal form of safety. Although each steamboat had a distinct sound, steamboats traveling with the current downstream had the right of way and were required to give one whistle blast, so both boats passed on their left or port sides. If a downstream steamboat gave two blasts of its whistle, it would pass on its right or starboard sides. When a moored vessel prepared for departure, it gave one long whistle blast and three short bursts as it departed. I can picture the steam pouring out of Kate Adams' boiler pipes into a clear blue sky while enjoying that deep bullfrog sound. It must have felt adventurous, romantic, and stimulating!

Over time, there were three *Kate Adams*: *Kate Adams* 1, 2, and 3. Number 1 was built in 1882 and was one of the first boats with electric lights. She sported luxury in each private cabin paneled with natural wood. Her beauty and luxury came to a sad end, though, in 1888, when she exploded and sank between Memphis and Helena. Fifty-five people lost their lives. Number 2 replaced her later in the year. She was more extensive than Kate I, but, at this time, the river traffic started to slow. It became difficult to make a satisfactory profit due to insufficient freight. As a result, she was sold and accidentally burned a few years later, in 1903. Number 3 was built in 1898. She was specially designed to navigate the river between Memphis, Helena, and Arkansas City. She became so popular that she appeared in the original movie *Uncle Tom's Cabin* of 1926, where she starred as *LaBelle Riviere*. Several scenes were filmed in

Helena, and local African Americans were cast as the maltreated enslaved people as part of the story, as well as 200 locals used in the mob scenes. Unfortunately, in 1927, she also burned. Number 3 was best referred to as "Lovin' Kate."

Now and then, a showboat would arrive in the port. Gambling, dancing, loud music, and minstrel shows were the attraction. The length of their stay depended on the participation of the locals, which could be anywhere from days to weeks.

Before the levee was raised to 60 feet, steamboats had a variety of places to dock in Helena. Some landed at the ends of Porter and Rightor Streets. Pecan Street was formerly a swamp fed by the river and curved around to Beech and York Streets. Refer to the plat map in chapter six to view the swamp area running through the middle of Helena as we know it today.

This area is now the replica site of Fort Curtis. Steamboats could travel up this far and dock when the river was high. Eventually, the swamp was filled with earth and turned into streets. Most of the land that filled this swamp came from the present-day location of the Baptist Church. It was the original location of Fort Curtis. This location was a high hill lowered with the dirt used to fill the swamp. One can sense the previous height of this area by viewing the present-day Solomon Playground. The playground was previously the location of the courthouse, referred to as the public square, as exhibited on the original plot map designed by Nicholas Rightor in 1820.

Also of note is the original Fort Curtis, constructed on the previous site where Sylvanus Phillips owned his house and where he and his daughter Helena Phillips were buried. His remaining daughter, Caroline Phillips Hanly, retained the property until 1874 when she sold off parts of it as lots. The Union used this area to construct Fort Curtis. Caroline Phillips Hanly and her husband sympathized with and supported the Union because they had the most to lose in material wealth under the Confederacy.

Modoc landing between Helena and Elaine was another popular boarding site for passengers traveling to Memphis. As stated earlier, it was also a favorite landing for out-of-state hunters. In her story about Elaine, Arkansas, Willie Mae Countiss Kyte wrote, "If you wanted a leisurely trip to Memphis, you caught the *Kate Adams* at Modoc landing. What an experience to be met by Captain Hodges and to enjoy the luxury of the Queen of the Riverboats. It was wonderful to stand on the upper deck, watch the roustabouts shuffle up and down the gangplank in perfect rhythm to the roustabout chant, visit with friends, and then go to your very nice stateroom to get ready for the delicious meal always served on the *Kate Adams*. You might sit out on the deck and enjoy the river, listen upstairs to the music, or dance to the band always on hand."

She refers to W.C. Handy, one of the most famous blues artists ever. He spent much time playing on *Kate Adams* 3 and established his career. Today, he is remembered and revered at the King Biscuit Blue Festival (KBBF), held every October in Helena, and attracts thousands worldwide.

Napoleon, Arkansas, was another famous landing for steamboats but was considered more of a frontier town because of an influx of land speculators, criminals, mosquitoes, and floodings. It was located at the mouth of the Arkansas River near where it entered the Mississippi in Desha County. Early on, because of its location, speculators saw the potential for it to grow to the likes of St. Louis or New Orleans. In 1837, Napoleon was chosen by the surgeon general as a place to build a marine hospital funded by the federal government to provide health accessibility for river travelers. In his memoir *Life on the Mississippi*, Mark Twain mentioned, "a town where I used to know the prettiest girl." Unfortunately, flooding prevented the construction of the hospital, while several undesirable residents allowed the town's buildings to deteriorate. Union troops took over the area in 1862 because most residents had abandoned it. Finally, by 1868, the Mississippi River's current had washed away Napoleon. Today, only a state historical marker remains in nearby McGehee. Napoleon is no longer listed on the current state maps.

Steamboats received their power from large heated boilers filled with water. Once the water boiled, it produced a vapor. The steam, or vapor, was then pumped into a cylinder, causing a piston to move upward to its top, where a valve opened to release the steam. After the steam was released, the piston would retreat to the bottom of the cylinder and repeat the process. This continuous action caused the boat's paddlewheel, which was attached to the piston, to turn. The turning motion of the paddlewheel propelled the steamboat as it was partially submerged in the water. Most of the earliest steamboats were fired with wood, but coal became their source as technology progressed because it burned much slower.

Explosions of steamboats were a common occurrence for a good part of the 1800s. By 1870, nearly 7,000 people had died along the Mississippi River and its tributaries due to at least 100 explosions. Excessive amounts of heat pumped into faulty or improperly constructed boilers or pumps made from pieces of low-quality cast iron were usually the cause, along with low water level in the boiler. There were reports of passengers being thrown for great distances and others being killed due to flying metal shards from the exploded boiler. Fires were common once the explosion developed because the boats were made of wood, and many people drowned or were severely injured.

Because so many people were severely burned and scalded in steamboat explosions, two eminent physicians developed a remedy to save and restore a person's health. They claimed, "For extensive burns or scalds, take soot from a chimney where wood was burned, rubbing it fine, and mixing one part soot to three parts of fresh grease that was not salted and spreading it on linen or muslin or any cotton cloth and placing it over the scalds. If the burn or scald was extensive, the cloth should be cut into stripes before putting it over the scald. Let the remedy be freely and fully applied, covering all the burned parts perfectly. No other application was required until the patient was well, except to apply new applications of the soot and lard, etc. In steamboat explosions, the remedy should, in nearly all cases, be at once applied, and if done, many valuable lives would be saved. A vast amount of suffering alleviated." Ouch! It sounds more like witchcraft to me!

One such explosion occurred when the *Pennsylvania* exploded near Memphis on June 13, 1858. Samuel Clemens, a.k.a. Mark Twain, and his younger brother Henry boarded in New Orleans to head north. Samuel was a cub pilot at the time under the leadership of the captain, Pilot William Brown. In his book *Cub Pilot on the Mississippi,* Clemens told how he got into an altercation with Pilot Brown and left the boat. His brother Henry remained on board, hoping to secure a job to become the purser. As *Pennsylvania* was nearing Ship Island, just south of Memphis, it exploded, killing 250 people. Henry Clemens died a few days later due to injuries he suffered. Samuel always said the dispute saved his life.

I remember my mother using a pressure cooker in the 1940s and 1950s. They had become a common household item for preparing meals during this period because they saved homemakers precious time while cooking. I also remember Mother being very nervous while using the cooker. It was equipped with a gauge exposing the rising temperature of the steam contained within it. The pressure caused the cooker to chatter and vibrate when the steam was released. As an adult, I now understand Mother's fear of a possible explosion as the temperature rose to over 250 degrees. She was born in 1911 and lived her entire life along the banks of the Mississippi, so I'm sure she was familiar with the consequences of a steam explosion.

Probably the most disastrous steamboat explosion ever to occur at Helena was *General Brown* in November of 1838. The reported number of deaths has differed over the years, but counts of between 25 and 55 have been recorded, as well as 75 injured. This incident also included several people who drowned when they jumped overboard.

General Brown was southbound from Louisville to New Orleans with 150 passengers, while other accounts report it carried 300 passengers. It was its first season trip, and the Ohio and Mississippi Rivers were very low.

Chronicles report that the Ohio River was only five feet deep, and the Mississippi's depth was seven feet. When the boat backed away from the dock in Louisville, it made contact with a sandbar and collided with the steamboat *Washington* heading upstream to Cincinnati, damaging one of the wheels. *General Brown* continued southbound with only one wheel working while the onboard carpenter repaired the other. It was not clear how many days it took to fix the wheel or if both boilers continued to be fired and filled with steam while only one wheel worked. In those days, there were no government regulations. The owners made all such inspections of their vessels.

It's hard to visualize any of the main rivers being this low today because of the levees and the dredging, which fall under the regulatory controls of the Corp of Engineers.

History records the Arkansas River being so low in the 1830s that steamboats couldn't travel from the Mississippi River to Little Rock. There were buildups of trees and branches washed away from the shore, becoming massively wedged together and interrupting the channels of larger boats.

During other seasons, the abundance of water became a curse. Crops were flooded in the fields and lost before they could be harvested. The annual spring flood of the Mississippi also presented problems for steamboats in establishing suitable docks to handle their cargo.

In 2023, I traveled to Louisville to see the Ohio River firsthand. I was shocked by its size. I had no idea it was so large. Its width at Louisville is larger than that of the Mississippi River in Memphis or Helena. The Ohio feeds into the Mississippi, as do several other rivers across the country. I had always heard the term "the mighty Mississippi." Naturally, growing up on its banks, I assumed no other river could rival its width and depth, especially its current, because so many other waterways fed into it.

The Mississippi is deeper today than in 1838 due to years of extensive dredging. Growing up in Helena in the 1950s, it was common to see the dredging machines working up and down the Mississippi. I assume the same has happened along the Ohio River, too. There is no way today that either river could be only seven feet deep again. Even as late as 1878, Congress authorized the four-and-a-half-foot channel for the Mississippi. In 1907, the depth was changed to six feet; in 1930, a nine-foot depth was approved.

General Brown was known to be one of the fastest boats on the river. Passengers said the steamboat *Empress* had trailed the *Brown* the morning of the explosion and was behind it as it docked in Helena. Unlike most steamboat explosions along the river, this occurred while moored at the dock, without the wheels churning. Supposedly, insufficient steam had been released to relieve pressure on the boilers. While *General Brown* was at the pier, several Helenians had gone aboard for a tour. That's when one of the boilers exploded, instantly killing Captain Samuel James Clark, some crew members, several passengers, and five Helenians. *The Macon Intelligencer* newspaper reported that his body was thrown 100 yards onto the bank. The exploding boiler landed on the bank, and the other boiler caused a fire aboard.

Many conflicting opinions and statements were not uncommon during this era.*The Macon Intelligencer* writes that even though steamboat regulations were not well enforced, " *General Brown* had on board the certificate of the inspectors who had examined her machinery stating she was safe." It continues to say, "There is an injunction in the late law in relation to steamboats requiring them to open the safety valve on stopping for the purpose of discharging or taking on cargo, fuel or passengers."

When the trailing *Empress* saw what had happened, it immediately pulled into the shore to help. Its' Captain John W. Russel and crew rushed aboard the *General Brown*. Survivors began to shout that powder was on board, and those capable started a bucket bigrade to extinguish the flames. During this process, they learned six negroes were in the forecastle and proceeded to rescue them. Captain Samuel James Clark was 38 years old and left his pregnant wife and three young children in Madison, Indiana. He was buried in the city cemetery, later called Graveyard Hill, today known as Reservoir Hill.

Below is a more detailed description of the event published in *Lloyds Steamboat Directory and Disasters*.

> EXPLOSION OF THE GEN. BROWN, NOVEMBER 25, 1838.
>
> For the particulars of this disaster, we are indebted to Capt. Robert McConnell, now of Paducah, Ky., was the clerk on board the General Brown and an eye-witness

of the explosion and its dreadful results. This steamer, under the command of Captain Clark, left Louisville, Ky., for New Orleans on November 19, 1838. This was her first trip of the season, and the water was quite low in both rivers, being only five feet in the Ohio and seven feet in the Mississippi. Circumstances seemed to threaten misfortune from the very beginning of the voyage; for in passing over a sandbar at no great distance from Louisville, the General Brown came in collision with the steamer Washington, bound up the river, by which accident the larboard wheel of the Gen. Brown was damaged to that degree that repairs were necessary before the boat could proceed. The carpenter succeeded in fitting up a temporary wheel, which answered the purpose very imperfectly; however, the boat was enabled to continue her trip, working along slowly until the morning of Sunday, November 25, when she reached Helena, Ark., where she stopped to land a passenger. This being done, the captain, who stood on the hurricane roof, took the bell-rope in his hand to give the usual signal of departure; but at the first tap of the bell, the boilers exploded with a deafening crash, and that single stroke of the bell was to many a signal of departure to that eternal world from whence no traveler returns. Capt. Clark himself, while still grasping the bell rope convulsively in his hand, was blown overboard, together with a portion of the woodwork on which he stood. He had been holding a lively conversation with Dr. Price, of Lexington, a few moments before. Dr. P. stood on the same platform, and shared the same melancholy fate, both gentlemen being afterwards found among the dead. Captain McConnell, who gives this account, was thrown from the railing on which he stood after notifying the captain that the boat was ready to start. He fell on the deck and received but little in-

> jury. He supposes that the persons killed numbered about fifty-five, and the wounded fifteen or twenty. The names which follow are all that he could call to remembrance.
>
> KILLED. —Capt. Samuel Clark, master of the boat; Joseph Underwood, and Hamilton McRay, pilots; James Wilson, first engineer; Basil Boons, mate; Ely Johns, second clerk; carpenter, name not recollected; Patrick Dunn, bar-keeper; eight or ten firemen and deckhands. Passengers—C. Libley, D. L. Davis, N. A. Miller, and Dr. Price, of Lexington, Ky.; H. M. Blanchard, E. Hubbard, George Johnson, J. K. Gutherite, T. D. Sims, C. Keane, T. D. Levey, A. Dugan, Dr. Johnson and wife, B. Walker, C. Stansbury, O. Perry, and several others, making a total of fifty-five. The names of the wounded are not given. Capt. McConnell exonerates the commander of the General Brown from all blame, declaring that he frequently urged the firemen and engineers to use the utmost caution, and to carry as little steam as possible, on account of the crippled condition of the boat.

There were different stories about the same incident reported by competitive companies. *The York Gazette* (York, PA) blamed the captain, while other newspapers focused on the human side and expressed sympathy for their crew and families. *The York Gazette* inferred that the captain was only interested in racing on the river. The same article stated that the Steamboat *Empress* developed a leak in a flat bottom boat it had in tow loaded with 50 horses; *General Brown* assisted by taking 30 of these horses on board.

The Southern Sun newspaper reported that steam was not adequately released as required but retained and exploded when the machinery was set into motion. It blames the crew because of "its reckless spirit of emulation and wantonness on the part of the officers by piling in wood to beat the *Empress*."

A letter published by the *Memphis Enquirer* on November 30, 1838, sent by Dr. J.B Prescott, said, "This accident, and all its consequences, are justly chargeable to the boat's officers. She never blew off steam during her stop, and the furnaces were twice filled up—so say the survivors. She was about to round out to give us chase." Dr. Prescott was on board the *Empress* and witnessed the terrible disaster.

A Letter from Benedict & Carter in Louisville, owners of *General Brown*, dated October 25, 1839, to Captain Clark's widow, said this. "We met Mr. McCallister, who was on board the *General Brown* at the time of the accident. His statement is fully confirmed by letters from Mr. R. McConnell, the boat clerk." They write, "One consolation we find ourselves is that there is no blame to be attached to any part of the crew. There was no want of knowledge of their business—nor neglect of duty. The Browns crew were all good men and well qualified for their different stations—and mostly of Capt. C's selection."

A letter written by R. McConnell to Captain Samuel Clark on September 8, 1838, mailed from Cincinnati said. "You went over the river the other morning before I had an opportunity of talking to you about going on the Genl Brown as Clerk. I thought I would 'wright' you a few lines when I arrived at Cincinnati, and if you want me to go on him, I will go. I had to come to Cincinnati to settle the old business, which I will get through within a few days then I will return to Louisville and see you thare. Mr. Carr is out of a berth and would like to go with you if you have no other person in view. Yours Respectfully Robt. McConnell."

One of my main objectives in traveling to Louisville in 2023 was to search for possible lawsuits concerning the explosion of *General Brown* in 1838. Not being a lawyer and reading such accounts and letters discouraged me from digging too deep into any recorded suits 185 years old. I am still looking to discover any information in previous internet searches, but I found many stories describing courthouse archives being lost due to fires. Also discouraging is the fact that most of these types of documents were not kept or scribed. The very fact that the explosion of *General Brown* is unknown to most residents of Helena gives me confidence that no suits were ever filed.

General Brown was named after Jacob Jennings Brown of Bucks County, Pennsylvania (May 9, 1775-February 24, 1828). He was an American army officer during the War of 1812, where he reached the rank of general and became a national hero due to his success. During the war, his recognition began after fending off the Canadian and British troops at Sackets Harbor, New York. In 1813, he led his troops in a total defeat of the British in the Second Battle of Sackets Harbor. It was an essential military shipyard where American naval vessels were constructed and used to protect the Great Lakes.

On July 3, 1814, exactly one day shy of 49 years, before the Battle of Helena in Arkansas on July 4, 1863, General Brown successfully directed his troops to recapture Fort Erie. This battle was considered a draw, as both sides withdrew, but it stopped the advancement of the British. The Americans destroyed the fort, preventing any further gains for the British.

In his early military life, he was the military secretary to Alexander Hamilton, one of the United States' founding fathers. This connection served him well in his postwar years as President James Monroe appointed him to be the nation's commanding general, where he established the General Recruiting Service. Today, it is known as The United States Army Recruiting Command (USAREC). Currently, this military branch employs 15,000 people who enlist, train, and provide leadership to our armed forces.

Although General Jacob Jennings Brown is unknown to most Arkansans, he became a national hero and was awarded the Congressional Gold Medal. Several cities across the nation are named after him. They are in Illinois, Indiana, Ohio, Wisconsin, Pennsylvania, and Tennessee. A monument stands at his gravesite in Washington, D.C., and an obelisk, located on the Arkansas state capitol grounds, honoring veterans from the War of 1812 buried in Arkansas. As referred to in chapter six, some of these veterans were awarded land grants for their service. So, it was only befitting that a steamboat be named after him.

Sources:

Phillips County Historical Quarterly Vol 6 No. 2, Vol 23 No. 1 & 2, Vol 8 No.1, Vol 17 No. 4, Vol 19 No. 1, 2, 3 & 4, Vol 2 No.4
Steamboat.org
Howardseamboatmuseum.org
Stltoday.com
Goodspeed Publishing Company, *History of Phillips County, Arkansas*
Lloyd's Steamboat Directory and Disasters On the Western Waters, Cincinnati, Ohio; James T. Lloyd & Co, 1856, pages 114-115
en.m.wikipedia.org Jacob Brown
armyhistory.org
sos.arkansas.gov Arkansas State Capitol Self-Guided Grounds tour
wonderopolis.org What is a steamboat
mywarof1812.com Major General Jacob Brown
nwaoline.com, remembering Napoleon by Tom Dillard
Encyclopedia of Arkansas, Napoleon (Desha County)
En.m.wikipedia.org, Napoleon, Arkansas
En.wikipedia.org, Pennsylvania (steamboat)
Cub Pilot on the Mississippi by Mark Twain
twainquotes.com
Macon Intelligencer, December 12, 1838, newspapers.com
Kentucky Gazette, June 27, 1839, newspapers.com
Carroll County Heritage Center Collection

Chapter Eleven

HATTIE ON THE HILL

When the body was unearthed on our playground in the 1950s, our parents were wise to be worried about diseases. I remember fear and discussions of yellow fever in particular. My memory eludes me as to why there was such a fear of yellow fever at this time, as I'm sure it was common knowledge that mosquitos caused it. Nevertheless, yellow fever was widely discussed by frightened parents and terrified children. I can only assume that the odd skin color of the body lying in a creepy coffin may have infused wild theories and conjectures.

Parents also were talking about the large number of deaths caused by the Spanish Flu when they were young. Naturally, this caused them to fear that the coffin might contain an infected body. The burial case looked nothing like the caskets of the present day. One of my friends says he remembered Doctor McCarty being called to come up to Reservoir Hill and make an inspection.

The history of yellow fever in Boston in 1693 and other cities during the 18th and 19th centuries, particularly along the southern coastal areas, carried guarded worries. I mentioned earlier that I remembered the body as brown-skinned. Yellow fever, by name, refers to jaundice or yellow skin discoloration. My parents also feared remnants of the Spanish Flu of 1918-1920. In the 1920s, they were approximately the same age as I was in the 1950s. They knew 50 million people worldwide had been infected and 675,000 had died in the United States, far more significant than the 175,000 lost to yellow fever. Looking back, a bit of hysteria had taken over the neighborhood.

Some people called the Spanish Flu the "three-day fever" because it struck so fast and viciously, causing muscle and joint pain, headache, dry throat, and chest pains with severe coughs. Another sign was a blueish tint of the skin. The disease caused temperatures to rise to around 104 degrees, and the infected person succumbed to viral pneumonia. The pneumonia was so severe that it caused the lungs to fill with fluid, resulting in hemorrhaging. Expiration was usually followed instantaneously or within a few hours.

Most people thought the spread of this deadly yellow fever disease was solely from person to person and contagious, much like COVID-19. In the 1800s, some doctors and scientists figured out mosquitoes caused it and recommended blanketing urban areas with a cloud of thick choking smoke. The smoke was created by burning tar, which reduced the number of new cases, but the side effects of unhealthy air caused other problems for the public.

Those who contracted yellow fever suffered headaches, muscle pain, nausea, high fever, jaundice, and vomiting. Within a couple of days, the fever attacked the internal organs of the liver and kidneys, causing internal bleeding. Some writings tell of a vile black vomit, thought to be infected blood. Most people died within seven days to ten days. Those few who survived developed an immunity from further infections.

Some of the infected were treated with bloodletting for a while, as it was felt this would rid people of the disease. It wasn't until 1905 that it was confirmed that mosquitoes transmitted the disease. It took until 1930 before a preventive vaccine was found, but there was no cure. It wasn't until 1951 that Max Theiler was awarded the Nobel Prize in Medicine for developing the virus vaccine. Thankfully, today, a single dose of the vaccine provides lifelong protection.

Still, there are around 200,000 annually reported cases of yellow fever worldwide, resulting in some 30,000 deaths. Most of these cases are reported in East, West, and Central Africa. Poor people mainly inhabit these areas of the world. The World Health Organization is making inroads by providing vaccinations and decreasing infections. However, the poverty in these stricken areas has added other problems because of political instability and insecurity. Their lists of diseases are COVID-19, Ebola, cholera, meningitis, malaria, monkeypox, chikungunya, leishmaniasis, and cVDP2. I don't know how people living in the wealthier parts of the world can complain about anything.

1853, yellow fever turned New Orleans into the "City of the Dead." It was recorded as the worst year on record, having 8,000 deaths. The rage flourished because of its warm, humid climate and contaminated cisterns. Slavery and immigration played a huge factor due to the social structure of the city's government. White people portrayed enslaved people as immune because of their skin color and because they were used to working outside in the heat. The influx of immigrants was a liability because they had no immunity and had not previously been exposed to the disease. The fever killed practically half of the infected people, but those who survived became immune. Some old wives' tales caused a lot of misunderstanding and even caused more losses.

For example, some immigrants tried to contract the fever, thinking they would recover and thus become immune. If they were successful, they would have an edge in the job market because employers were looking for healthy people to hire due to a labor shortage. Plantation owners tried to round up Black people acclimated to the disease by paying 25 to 50 percent more in wages.

Two years later, in 1855, yellow fever found its way into Helena through a "steamer" that came upriver from New Orleans. The city's population was only 1,500, so the fever hit the city hard. When the fever broke out on the steamer, members of the Burnett family contracted it. They were the first reported cases entering Helena when the steamer docked.

Their mother, Martha, was a poor widow with four children trying to provide the best way she knew for her family. She was 28 and had daughters Martha, 15, Harriet (Hattie), age 11, and sons William, 14, and Oscar, 9. William was a newsboy selling papers aboard the steamer, while Martha supported her family with her needle. I presume this meant she sewed.

Hattie succumbed to the fever and died a few days later, as well as a few other passengers. It was reported that another girl aboard, no name given, age 14, also "died with the black vomit." The rest of the Burnett family recovered. I find no record of where Hattie was buried. I can only assume the city of Helena permitted her to be buried in the city cemetery because of her family's hardship and past documented stories of burials.

As told in a previous chapter, the city of Helena purchased acreage and formally developed Evergreen Cemetery. Later, the name was changed to Maple Hill. In 1870, known bodies were moved from the city cemetery to Evergreen Cemetery. Hattie Burnett was not among those listed. Naturally, this has made her a candidate as the lady in the coffin considering the date of 1848 for the first made Fisk coffins.

The first cases of yellow fever hitting Helena after the steamer arrived from New Orleans sent panic through the city. People started fleeing to the country for safety. City authorities requested people to remain in Helena to help with the disaster, to care for the sick, and to bury the dead. Only three doctors were in town then; one contracted the fever early on. This situation only left the two doctors. Only three citizens stepped forward to help. They were Mr. Rice, a Methodist preacher; Patrick Cleburne, a druggist aged 22; and Thomas Hindman. These men were not medically trained, but they made around-the-clock visits to help the remaining citizens by purchasing food and supplies with their money to help wherever needed. They made themselves present and placed the lives of others above their own.

Thomas Hindman had previously been involved in politics in Mississippi and moved to Helena to practice law during the 1850s. He and Patrick Cleburne had become friends. Cleburne was originally from Ireland but served three years in the British Army. He moved to the United States and became a naturalized US citizen in 1855. He loved Helena and his new country. He became involved in many community projects. In time, they later served in the Confederate Army. Both were eventually promoted to General and became two of seven generals to serve from Helena. Their leadership skills were evident in their dedication to helping others during the yellow fever panic.

Cleburne sided with the Southern states when the talk of secession peaked. He was not a fan of slavery but claimed affection for the Southern people because they claimed him as one of their own. In 1863, he sensed the defeat of the Confederacy and proposed to emancipate the enslaved people. He suggested that emancipation did not have to include Black equality, but it would secure Southern independence under reasonable orders. Naturally, his Southern counterparts rejected his thoughts and, in most cases, vigorously attacked them. In November 1864, he died in the Battle of Franklin, Tennessee. He was buried in nearby Columbia, Tennessee, where his remains were interred for six years. In 1870, his body was returned to his adopted hometown of Helena, Arkansas, and placed in the Confederate Cemetery above Maple Hill Cemetery.

The people of Helena remembered his unselfish acts of helping the citizens during the yellow fever panic. He was respected and admired as a citizen and military leader. Author Shelby Foote says he was the best division commander on either side serving in the American Civil War. He was known and adored by his men. The following article, found on historicalmarketproject.com, follows.

> "**Bringing Cleburne Home**- on April 27, 1870, Leonard Mangum and Dr. Hector Grant journeyed from Arkansas to Tennessee to bring Cleburne home. In Memphis, black-plumed horses pulled the hearse from the railroad station to the wharf, draped in black crepe and decorated with green ribbons. Jefferson Davis and a host of other former Confederates marched in the procession. People lined the streets to say farewell to the fallen hero. "Never did Memphis exhibit such a solemn, impressive, and soul-moving scene," reported one newspaper.
>
> In Helena, the body lay in state at St John's Church. The city, awash in black crepe, closed for the

> day. A quarter-mile-long procession snaked from the church to Confederate Hill. Cleburne was home at last.
>
> **The Cleburne Memorial**
> The small headstone brought from Tennessee marked Cleburne's grave for twenty-one years. The Ladies Memorial Association tried erecting the memorial dedicated on May 10, 1891. The ceremony began at Helena's grand Opera House, and General James C. Tappan acted as master of ceremonies for speeches, poems, and songs. Scores of Confederate veterans, residents, and visitors marched to the cemetery. After speeches and prayers, five young women dressed in white, the daughters of Confederate Generals, unveiled the memorial."

Thomas Hindman was remembered for his bravery and assistance when yellow fever arrived in Helena. Also, a general from Helena shared many similar traits to his friend Patrick Cleburne. Although they differed in their views of slavery, they remained friends. Both men served the Confederacy well and will forever be remembered in Helena as dedicated soldiers and citizens. Each has been memorialized with very prominent monuments in the Confederate Cemetery. Patrick Cleburne died in battle at the young age of 36, and Thomas Hindman at the age of 40. His death occurred after the war when he was murdered with an assassin's bullet.

Sources:

Who.int, World Health Organization
Pbs.org, Historical Guide to Yellow Fever
Pbs.org, American Experience
Cdc.gov>yellowfever
Aarchives.gov, The Deadly Virus
Library.missouri.edu, Spanish Flu in Columbia

History.com, Spanish Flu
Phillips County Historical Quarterly, Vol 2 No. 2
Npr.org., How yellow fever turned New Orleans into the City of the Dead
en.wikipedia.org wiki Patrick Cleburne
historicalmarkerproject.com/markers/HM21G7_back-to-HM21G7.html
who.int
en.m.wikipedia.org Thomas Carmichael Hindman Jr.
Odyssey, *The Way of Love* by Scott Gunn

Chapter Twelve

SECRETS OF THE *SULTANA*

If Hattie Burnett's body was unrecoverable by being left on Graveyard Hill due to the destroyed tombstones, then her spirit had a prime view of all the river traffic passing by on the Mighty Mississippi for at least 100 years. The *Sultana* was the most famous but the least discussed event, which could have shared many secrets between the living and the dead.

Of all the sidewheel steamboats, the *Sultana's* sinking was the most underreported in riverboat history. Her explosion on April 27, 1865, was the worst maritime disaster ever in the United States. This disaster ranks fourth in world history in terms of lives lost on the water.

On the *Titanic, 1,513* people died when it sank in 1912. Many were Americans. But, as many as 1,800 casualties, including known dead and missing Americans, were aboard the *Sultana* when the boat exploded on the Mississippi River. (Other reports say only 1,169 people perished.)

This lack of recognition for this tragic event began with the ending of the Civil War on April 9, 1865, when Robert E. Lee of the Confederacy surrendered to Union General Ulysses S. Grant at Appomattox Courthouse in Virginia. A few days later, on April 14, 1865, John Wilkes Booth assassinated President Abraham Lincoln while he attended a play at Ford's Theater in Washington, D.C. The President died the following day, April 15, 1865, at 7:22 a.m.

The news of the *Sultana* disaster was overshadowed by the ending of the American Civil War, President Abraham Lincoln's assassination, and the quest to apprehend John Wilkes Booth. Also, the public had become accustomed to hearing reports about many significant battlefield losses. Some rumors also claimed the Confederates had sabotaged her. Because so much was taking place, the story of the *Sultana* was not at the top of the news cycle.

During this short 12-day period, news traveled slowly. The fastest communications traveled only by telegraph, but most southern states were cut off because of the war. As the information did reach the south, the prisoner-of-war camps at Andersonville, Georgia, and Cahaba, Alabama, began to release Union prisoners. Cahaba held nearly 3,000 prisoners in a 15,000-square-foot stockade area. Confederate Captain Howard A.M. Henderson was in charge and possessed solid Methodist beliefs. He was remembered for his kindness under the circumstances, while around 145 prisoners died due to the conditions. The treatment in the Civil War prisons was despicable because of the living conditions. Still, Cahaba was considered one of the more humane prison camps, with fewer deaths than any of the other prisons.

Cahaba was near Selma and was once the state capital of Alabama from 1819 to 1826. It was regarded as a thriving antebellum town, but after the war, it was abandoned. Today, it is known as Old Cahawba Archaeological Park. Some chronicles report that 9,000 prisoners passed through the camp.

Andersonville was a completely different story. It was located in Sumter County, Georgia, and thus named Camp Sumter. The compound was the shape of a parallelogram, 779 feet by 1,620 feet, surrounded by a stockade wall. Each side had a 19 feet wide trench within the enclosure, which prisoners could not enter. If they did, the guards had orders to shoot them. Andersonville was built to accommodate 10,000 POWs but usually held around 26,000 soldiers. Frequently, it held up to 33,000 men. Thirteen thousand died due to poor sanitation, malnutrition, disease, overcrowding, and exposure. The only source of drinking water was a creek, which also served as the latrine, filled with fecal matter. The filthy sanitary conditions resulted in dysentery and typhoid fever, expediting the demise of many prisoners. The lack of food rations, warm clothing, and firewood also added to the inhumane conditions.

After the war, Captain Henry Wirz, the stockade commander, was arrested for murder. He was found guilty by a military tribunal and hanged on November 10, 1865. He was one of a few Confederate officials charged with violating the rules of war. U.S. officials tried to prove he was following the orders of his ranking officers but failed to do so. Wirz argued that he was being hanged for following such orders but suffered the consequences of war crimes.

Today, Andersonville National Historic Site is a burial reminder of the treatment of captured Union soldiers of the Civil War. It is now open to accepting all deceased U.S. prisoners of any war for burial. The National Prisoner of War Museum is located at this site, too.

By March 20, 1865, only a few weeks before the end of the war, the Union and Confederacy had agreed to a prisoner exchange to include some of those from Cahaba and Andersonville. Those released started their journey back home to the North by arriving at Camp Fisk, the Union Headquarters in Vicksburg. They traveled by boat, some by train, and others by foot. Most were exhausted, injured, and hungry after the trip and weary from being away from home for such a long time fighting the war. Vicksburg was the port city in Mississippi and was designated as a place for them to catch steamboats to take them to the Ohio, Tennessee, and Missouri rivers for a final trip home. River travel was the most logical way to reach home due to the destruction of many railroad tracks caused by the war and the lack of roads.

When the captain of the steamboat *Sultana,* James Cass Mason, learned about the surrender at Appomattox Courthouse in Virginia, he was in Cairo, Illinois. He was aware of the prisoners who were released at Vicksburg, Mississippi. Seeing an opportunity to make a quick profit, he headed the *Sultana* south toward Vicksburg. The U.S. federal government had announced it would pay steamboat captains $5 for every soldier and $10 for every officer transported back north.

Upon arriving in Vicksburg, Captain Mason met Colonel Ruben Hatch, the Chief Quartermaster of the Department of Mississippi. Captain Mason tells Colonel Hatch he must go to New Orleans to pick up some commercial passengers and cargo before heading back north.

The two agreed to load as many soldiers as possible on the *Sultana* and split the profits. When the *Sultana* arrived back in Vicksburg, the chief engineer discovered one of the boilers was damaged and needed repair. Captain Mason was told it would take nearly a week and refused to wait that long. He convinced the boiler company to make a temporary patch job. He said he would return to Vicksburg later to have the boiler fully repaired after the soldiers were delivered to Cairo, Illinois.

The Sultana's legal capacity was 376 passengers, and she carried an 85-person crew. Her length was 260 feet, about 640 feet shorter than a football field. The temptation to load as many people as possible was too great for Captain Mason and Colonel Hatch to pass up a chance to split an enormous, easy profit. The steamboat was overloaded with approximately 2,500 people in an almost standing-room-only situation.

The patch job repair was still in process as people were boarding. After departing, the *Sultana* started her trip north against the flooded spring thaw and cold waters. She stopped for more supplies when she made it to Helena, Arkansas, where photographer Thomas Bankes noticed her overloaded. As he took the picture, most passengers moved to one side of the steamboat, causing it to list. He took his picture on April 26, 1865, about 7 a.m. By 1 a.m., the *Sultana* had reached Memphis, Tennessee, where it coaled and loaded on more cargo. She then departed for the last leg of her trip, heading to Cairo, Illinois. After traveling only a few miles north of Memphis, near Marion, Arkansas, the patched boiler exploded because of the extra weight and pushing against the rapid downstream current of the cold waters of the Mississippi River.

Bankes' iconic picture has forever linked Helena as part of the history of the *Sultana*. Banks resided in Helena in 1860 and opened a photography studio in 1862. He specialized in portraits but went on to capture many images of soldiers and enslaved people.

There have been several theories as to what caused the explosion. There were reports that the repaired boiler didn't explode but remained intact. Another was that the engineer was drunk, incapacitated, and unable to function correctly. The sabotage theory carried a lot of weight because of the recent war ending in favor of the Union. Still, it was reported that many Confederate soldiers worked to help save survivors, and it was later dismissed purely as a rumor. Ultimately, the excess weight and insufficient water in the boilers were to blame.

A chain reaction caused the other boilers to crack and fall onto the deck, engulfing the boat in flames while the wheelhouse broke away partially from the side, putting the steamboat into a spin. Several people were killed instantly. Others jumped into the icy water and drowned, while others suffered lifelong injuries and later died. A few hung onto the boats' floating debris and drifted down to sand bars, while others floated back down the river to Memphis. Reports say bodies turned up along the shores of the Mississippi for weeks, and some were never found. The overcrowded *Sultana* carried less than 80 life preservers and had only one lifeboat and a yawl.

No one was ever held accountable for the loss of so many lives caused by the disaster. Captain Mason died on board, and Captain Hatch resigned from the army when he found out about the tragedy because, as a private citizen, he could avoid court-martial.

In 1982, 117 years later, an archaeological expedition led by Jerry O. Potter of Memphis found the remnants of the *Sultana* buried 32 feet underground in a soybean field on the Arkansas side of the Mississippi River. After changing course many times, the river's main channel is about two miles from the original sinking.

History reveals itself as years pass, and new evidence is uncovered when people's interests are peaked, as is the case for the Sultana disaster. Because of other more prominent and overriding circumstances during 1865, the story of the catastrophe never received the attention it deserved and was forgotten. The same memories followed the explosion of *General Brown* in Helena, Arkansas, in 1838, 27 years earlier.

It wasn't until 2015 that artifacts and information were assembled and displayed in a small museum in Marion, Arkansas, the town closest to the event. The Disaster Museum, as it is named, has archived over 100 photos of passengers and crew aboard the steamboat, newspaper articles, and other related information. There is also an in-depth list of the soldiers aboard and recounts some of their stories. I especially found it interesting that a local citizen built a close replica of the *Sultana* on display. It, of course, is much smaller than the actual size of 260 feet. However, it presents an image of reality, allowing one to imagine what it must have been like aboard the overcrowded steamboat standing under the open sky in the cold weather. I can also visualize the continuous noise of the boilers and the turning of the sidewheel pushing back the waves as the boat pushes north against the swift current of the Mighty Mississippi River.

Finally, since 2015, the *Sultana* Historic Preservation Society has succeeded in receiving recognition through a congressional resolution to expand the museum. A groundbreaking ceremony occurred in November 2022 after a $6 million grant was approved. Another $4 million will be raised to install the exhibits once the building is finished. In 2021, Arkansas Gov. Asa Hutchinson said that $750,000 of state funds would be provided for the museum. Once finished, this will be an incredible historical museum. I have been to the original museum and can't wait to see the finished new exhibit.

The *Titanic* is the most remembered and famous marine disaster involving only one vessel. It has been well-published and recognized worldwide since 1912 when 1,513 people died. It was on its maiden voyage from Southampton, England, to New York City. It carried 2,224 passengers when it struck an iceberg in the North Atlantic Ocean; most passengers perished.

Many books have been written, and movies have relived the events. The fact that it was the largest and most modern passenger ship on the waters at the time added to the intrigue. Numerous fingers have been pointed over the years toward the mismanagement by the crew and captain. Luxury suites sold at $4,300 would equate to a cost of $122,000 today. It was advertised as unsinkable but sank on its maiden voyage. So, it's easy to understand why this is the most famous maritime disaster involving only one ship.

The *Wilhelm Gustloff* falls into a category similar to the *Sultana*. This luxury liner was the pride and joy of Adolf Hitler, with a capacity of 10,000 passengers. On January 30, 1945, it was attacked by a Russian submarine and sank after being hit by three torpedoes 12 nautical miles off present-day Poland. It was an act of wartime retaliation. The estimated loss of life is thought to be at least 9,000 German citizens, nearly four times the loss of lives on the *Titanic*. Strangely, the *Wilhelm Gustloff* was only about a third of the size of the *Titanic*. Because WWII was in process, the Nazis regime kept the event under wraps. As facts emerge, the *Wilhelm Gustloff* is now considered the deadliest maritime disaster involving a single vessel in history. Although *Wilhelm Gustloff* has nothing to do with Helena, the Mississippi River, steamboats, or explosions, I think it is an integral part of comparing history when considering the loss of human lives on waterways.

An interesting side story associated with this human tragedy involves the famous Amber Room, sometimes referred to as the "Eight Wonder of the World." It was designed and crafted by Germans and later gifted to the Russian Empire in the early 1700s in order to form an alliance with Tsar Peter the Great. During WWII, as Hitler was pillaging artwork from all over Europe, the Amer Room became a victim of German aggression. There are many stories and speculations as to what became of it, but as of today, nothing has been confirmed as to its whereabouts.

One such story was that when the Germans stole it, they packed it in crates and loaded it aboard the *Wilhelm Gustloff*. The Russians had been searching Europe for it for some time, but the Germans were determined to add it to their treasure trove of stolen masterpieces worth billions. It seems fitting that two bad-actor nations unknowingly destroyed what each badly wanted.

For many, the story of the *Sultana* is unfamiliar. Most Americans know nothing about it. But now we can remember this part of our past and honor those who died in the disaster. Different historical circumstances have prevented the *Sultana* from reaching notoriety. All of this should now change; its story will finally be told and looked on with pride as a vital part of our American history.

While exploring steamboats, I succumbed to an overwhelming feeling of nostalgia. I cannot continue writing without sharing my excitement. I must acknowledge my favorite steamboat, the *Arabia*.

Arabia perished under circumstances different from the other boats I have discussed, but its story is alive. I say this because I have walked on its deck and viewed the cargo it carried when it sank in the Missouri River on September 5, 1856.

The *Arabia* carried over 200 tons of cargo to be sold in general stores. It was headed north on the Missouri when it passed over a submerged tree snag. The snag punctured the hull, and the steamboat sank immediately.

To my surprise, the Missouri River is the longest in the United States. It is 2,341 miles long, and the Mississippi River, the second longest, is 2,202 miles long. The Missouri River is a tributary of the Mississippi, running through seven states beginning in Montana and flowing into the Mississippi at St. Louis, Missouri.

It remains a critical river today, providing drinking water for many communities and cooling water for power plants. It still serves the same purpose today, as an avenue for transporting goods and merchandise as it did over one hundred and fifty years ago. Today's difference is that those western faraway places were referred to as the frontiers back then. The combination of both rivers makes this river system the world's fourth longest, behind the Nile, Amazon, and Yangtze Rivers.

I toured the *Arabia* Steamboat in its museum in Kansas City, Missouri. It is a fascinating site since almost everything has been fully recovered, cleaned, and dried and is now being exhibited. The artifacts are neatly displayed in glass cases. Many originated from around the world and in this country before the war. Experts have proclaimed this the most extensive "pre-Civil War treasure collection."

Various tools, clothing, dinnerware, jewelry, food, keys, candles, matches, lamps, pistols, saddles, perfume, tobacco, buckles, medicine, buttons, beads, and buckets are displayed, and even some whiskey and jars of pickles! However, some of the whiskey was lost because it was in wooden barrels on the main deck and floated downstream. Everything else was recovered, just as it was when initially loaded on the boat in 1856. Viewing the cargo of the *Arabia* gave me a true sense of what was meant by a packet boat. One of the museum owners said he had eaten some of the preserved pickles, and they were fine, and he remained so, too.

The *Arabia*, unlike most steamboat accidents caused by explosions, filled with water rapidly once the tree stump punctured the hull. The stump that caused it to sink is also a part of the display. It was still lodged in the hull when the *Arabia* was salvaged and is one of the important artifacts. All 150 passengers aboard made it safely to shore. The only loss of life was a mule. The mule was tied to a railing when the *Arabia* sank, but the owner swore he had untied it so it could swim to shore. However, after the excavation of the event took place in 1988 (132 years after it sank), the skeleton of the mule was found still tethered to a railing. His skeleton remains are also on display.

Likewise, it is captivating to see how *Arabia* was located and brought back to life as a beautiful past exhibit. It was not just setting at the bottom of the Missouri River after 132 years because the river had changed course. David Hawley found it in a cornfield buried under 45 feet of dirt a half-mile from the river's main channel. He used a magnetometer to pinpoint the location.

Present in the museum is also a machine that dries and restores clothing. It's incredible to see hats, coats, shoes, and other apparel items over 150 years old still looking brand new. An excellent documentary tells the history, presents detailed pictures of the excavation, and recounts the entire story. Only a few treasures like this are seen today and can be accompanied by the details and the display of the recovered artifacts.

Sources:

en.m.wikipedia.org, Sultana (steamboat)
civilwarprisoners.com, Civil War Prisons
cahawba.com, Old Cahawba
nps.gov, History of the Andersonville Prison
en.m.wikipedia.org, Andersonville Prison
britannica.com, Anderson National Historic Site
marinersmuseum.org, Tragedy on the Mississippi

mshistorynow.mdah.ms.gov, Surviving the Worst: The Wreck of the Sultana at the End of the American Civil War
socialstudiesar.org, The Sultana Disaster Museum in Marion, Arkansas
Arkansas Democrat-Gazette, November 2022, Paige Eichkorn
en.m.wikipedia.org, sinking of the Titanic
history.com, The Wilhelm Gustloff
Phillips County Historical Quarterly, VOL 33 #3 & 4
Arabia Steamboat Museum
Mississippi River fact- Mississippi National River & Recreation Area (U.S. National Park Service.
Missouri River facts, Wikipedia
Smithsonian Magazine, Fergus M.Bordewich
Militaryhistorynow.com, The Gustloff Incident
Militaryimagesmagazine-digital.com
En.m.wikipedia.org/wiki/Amber Room

Chapter Thirteen

THE CURSE OF OAK ISLAND

I have enjoyed watching the TV program *The Curse of Oak Island* for a few years. It's presented seasonally on the History Channel, telling the story of two brothers who grew up in Michigan. As kids, they were fascinated with finding lost treasures. A story they began following in *Readers Digest* became a lifelong search for treasure buried on Oak Island in Nova Scotia around 1795. After years of watching them search and not discover the mother lode, I still enjoy seeing them uncover small bits and pieces of related relics and artifacts. I am eager to see them locate the main treasure, which they say is buried in The Money Pit. It's fascinating to see everything they do unearth as each new episode offers extensive details of their searches. They don't give up but keep running upon new clues. The most used phrase by the narrator is "may be connected."

So, this is where I find myself, looking for the lady in the coffin. My search, though, is the reverse of theirs. I discovered what I was NOT looking for as a kid, but NOW I'm trying to unlock the secret of who she was, why she was there, and what happened to her. I started with nothing but memories that have been lodged in my brain since my days as an adolescent. Only now, in my golden years, have I found the time and resources to bring all my wonders and imaginations together and look for answers.

As a result, I have been down many rabbit holes. Some have been exhausting, and others have been surprising and informative. All have given me a greater sense of our country's development and the hardships our ancestors endured, allowing new generations to live better lives. Even more surprising is that I have found out more about myself.

Hattie Burnett (Hattie on the Hill) has been among the most enjoyable searches. Although she died at 11, her family history led me to see the progression of life in Helena and the Delta in those early years. It provided me with a different insight into how I view the past. Her family struggled to make a living, with her mother sewing and her older brother William, age 14, selling papers.

Newspaper clippings tell of William Burnett selling papers at age 14 to help support the family. The census data shows the Burnett family living together and having a real estate value of $1,000. As the 1860 census rolled around, their real estate value jumped to $3,000.

By then, William was in his early twenties and was still involved in selling newspapers. However, his hard work and ambition advanced his status to publisher. As a young boy, he served as an apprentice for the *Democratic Star* and *Southern Shield,* both early newspapers of Helena. It was common for several newspapers to be available simultaneously during those days.

By 1865, he had become the publisher of the *Western Clarion* and was doing well enough to place his brother in charge of it while he advanced his newspaper empire and founded the *Helena Weekly World* in 1871. A couple of years later, he founded the *Helena Daily Mail.* Still, his crowning achievement was establishing the *Helena World* in 1887 as one of Arkansas's most prominent papers after purchasing it from William R. Burke.

Somewhere during these years, William Burnett must have retrieved the remains of his little sister, Hattie. I find no records of this occurrence, but I have seen a picture of her final resting place in Maple Hill marked with a very fine tombstone. I see this only happening due to William Burnett's prestigious status. Because of this picture, Hattie Burnett was eliminated from my search.

Goodspeed Publishing characterized Burnett as being known for his "perseverance, enterprise, and progress, as well for many other admirable traits of character, and to a great extent, he enjoyed the esteem and confidence of his fellow man." All of this with only "acquiring a common school education." It is evident in the lovely marble tombstone he provided for his little sister, whom he never forgot.

The *Helena World* has been the most renowned and constant source of newspapers from Helena for years. Before he died in 1892, William Burnett sold the paper but did very well by leaving a named newspaper legacy for the city of Helena.

At one time, the *Helena World* was described as the oldest and longest-running newspaper West of the Mississippi. Over the years, its ownership has changed several times, but the names of Helena and World have remained in the title in some form. Despite the changing news market, TV, media, internet, etc., the paper has found a way to continue to exist.

William Burnett learned from a young age that the newspaper business was a valuable source of income. Even before he was born, many newspapers had existed and later failed in Helena. People followed the news and considered it an essential part of their lives. They found exciting articles in papers from wherever they were available. For example, The *Arkansas Gazette* published information on the death of Sylvanus Phillips in its November 10, 1830 issue. In 1831, it followed up with an article about his daughter Helena Phillips dying at age 15.

The *Constitutional Journal,* established in 1836, and The *Southern Shield,* founded in 1840, were also published in Helena, providing advertisements and news. The *Helena Herald* and The *Helena Democrat* provided political information for many followers. The *Constitutional* Journal changed its name to *The Helena Spy* in 1838 when it changed owners. Most of these papers were weekly publications, but other new publications still needed to be born. The *True Witness* was established in 1848 and was supported by the state's first female compositor. *The Bulletin* found its way onto the scene with its location in a bakery.

In 1854, a year before Hattie Burnett died, The *States Rights Democrat* was started. It was perhaps the most politically influential publication at the time. The founder was Virginius Hutchens, who had experience writing and publishing books. Later, Thomas C. Hindman became an editor. Hindman, of course, later became a congressman and then one of the seven generals from Helena during the Civil War. After the war, he was murdered as he was sitting in his house when someone shot him through an open window. No one was ever charged or caught for the crime, but there were rumors it was because of his political ties.

There were several other short-lived newspapers during the 1800s. *The Note-Book,* The *Helena Weekly Clarion, The Phillips County Democrat, The Herold,* and *The Shield.* A fraternal Negro weekly, *The Royal Messenger,* and *The Interstate Reporter,* a religious Negro weekly, also appeared.

In 1974, the *Helena World* published a Souvenir Section of the May 11, 1904 edition. This Souvenir Section edition covered decades of the growth of Helena in Phillips County with pictures and stories of successful businesses, from sawmills to funeral homes and more.

The most profitable industry back then was cotton. There were plenty of cotton mills and compress companies to process the tons of cotton raised in the surrounding areas of Helena. The descendants of the Hornor family were widely and deeply invested in cotton. Their involvement in cotton also produced a ripple effect for other industries. For example, cotton shipping helped the railroads and steamboats expand jobs and revenue. Banking and insurance companies began to emerge, drawing in qualified, experienced financiers and managers. Citizens were interested in saving, which led to the opening of Peoples Savings Bank and Trust Co. in 1889 with a then gigantic capital of $30,000. Judge John S. Hornor was involved in banking as early as 1872 and passed his business, the Bank of Helena, down to his son Sidney H. Hornor.

Major John J. Hornor also presided over a successful lumber plant making boxes and providing finished wood products for other plants. Most buildings in the last half of the 1800s and the first half of the 1900s were constructed of wood. The compress companies were stuffed with cotton, so insurance became profitable due to those highly flammable fibers.

Helena had a variety of small businesses, one of which was run by Joseph Truemper, who built and repaired furniture in a building 40 x 132 feet. He managed to succeed, but all businesses were significant. In 1888, Wooten & Smith started a mercantile house at the northwest corner of Cherry and Elm Streets, producing a quarter of a million annual income.

Dennis Keeshan knew how to make it big. He realized that most citizens would eventually become clients. So, he and Jordan Lambert opened a funeral home that provided burials and much more. Keeshan was an experienced blacksmith assistant and wagon maker. Jordan had experience in the dry goods business. Together, they provided all the necessary supplies, from coffins to carriages, for proper funerals. They supplied several other funeral homes across the state. Later, Ed Keeshan, Dennis's brother, joined the business. They began to provide full-service funerals, including the casket, hearse, funeral cars, gravesites, embalming, clothing, shaving, and washing and dressing the body. Other incidentals could be included upon request. I reviewed some of the funeral records at the state archives covering some 50 years. The number of funerals performed over those years was unbelievable, and the profits were considerable.

It was the birth of a city expanding into other businesses and jobs. They supported, provided, and fed off one another as they opened and started various factories, services, schools, churches, and utilities.

Descendants of various city founders remained in Helena for years. Following the Hornor family were such names as Neal, Harrington, Hargraves, Quarles, Nelson, Moore, Underwood, Burke, Merrifield, Short, Tappan, Mays, Straub, Wooten, Saia, Truemper, St. Columbia, Smith, Freeman, Lambert, Faulkner, Reeves, Clopton, Chew, Mitchell, Berton, Bush, Etoch, Tanner, Hanks, Isaacs, Mayer, Kelly, Clancy, Hickey, Jones, Epps, Key, Pillow, Solomon, Barlow, McRee, Rightor, Cohen, Palmer, Polk, Anderson, and Adams, only to mention a very few.

Many of these family names are historic for Helena. I grew up with several of them and their descendants, having no idea that their ancestors played vital roles in the city's development. At our young age, my friends also had no idea. Some of these names have been present for nearly 200 years, and these historical names still live there in many cases. In others, some of the families have died off or moved away. However, their contributions are recorded in many past newspapers or are still visible in some buildings, streets, landmarks, and history books.

Walking through various cemeteries in Helena, namely Maple Hill, Saint Mary's, and Temple Beth El, it's easy to spot numerous stones marked with familiar names. Some of the bodies were transferred from Graveyard Hill. Might it be that the lady in the coffin was a relative of one of the famous founders of Helena, or maybe she was an unknown, forgotten person?

Sources:

Phillips County Historical Quarterly VOL 10 # 2, VOL 26 # 1 & 2, VOL 33 #1 & 2, VOL 13 #1
Goodspeed Publishing Co., *Biographical and Historical Memoirs of Eastern Arkansas*
John 1:1 NIV

Chapter Fourteen

CONNECTING THE DOTS

Throughout most of my adult life, I have wondered what became of the dead lady I saw in the coffin when I was a kid. I often curiously schemed for ways to identify her and tell her story. I mistakenly assumed it would be simple! I imagined all I had to do was to locate a 1950s edition of the *Helena World* newspaper, and an article would appear detailing a bunch of kids unearthing an old-timey casket. Wrong! Wrong! Wrong!

I needed much more help pinpointing which year of the 1950s I had observed her body. I also learned that what we were viewing was not a casket but a coffin. One of my main memories is that the kudzu was dormant, as we couldn't play on the hill because it was taller than we were!

Between 1956 and 1959, I was between 13 and 16. As pointed out earlier, these were the glorious years when my friends and I spent endless hours on Reservoir Hill digging caves, having BB-gun wars, shooting slingshots, camping, swinging on grapevines, flying kites, and fantasizing about girls as we went through puberty. It was one of those years when the coffin experience interrupted all those priceless life experiences.

Looking through city annals, such as census, deeds, funerals, marriage, death, or military certificates, was a helpful place to search. I found all sorts of information online and at the library. The point is that much of the information might have been available if I knew where and how to look. Because of my inexperience, this has been a true learning adventure for me. It requires reading, connecting the dots, and following leads. But reading old newspapers, encyclopedias, and history books has also been a lot of fun.

The *Phillips County Historical Quarterly* has been one of my primary sources of information, and I have found many exciting stories about Helena. They have captured data on its origins, development, and growth, covering centuries and decades. Numerous features have led me to further study by subscribing to Ancestry, which has provided more relevant detailed information and facts. I have even connected descendants of people on Ancestry and made friends with them on *Facebook*.

After finally realizing I could not gather all the information and facts I needed before I began writing, I gave in and sat at the computer. I decided to start writing and explore as I went along. It has been a laborious process but very informative and enjoyable. When discussing my search, I have picked up new friends on *Facebook*, the Arkansas State Archives, the Butler Center for Arkansas Studies, and several other sources.

My lifelong friend Rudy Shultz is the administrator of *Helena Friends* on *Facebook*. He has been an avid researcher of Helena's history for years and has fed me information whenever he locates something I can use. Rudy allowed me to post a picture of a coffin, hoping to shake out anyone who may have remembered this event when we were kids. Bingo! It was a great start. Several people replied that they remembered just as I did. I found it fascinating how many responded. Many were my age, some a few years younger or older. I was shocked that many lived in totally different neighborhoods, nowhere near Reservoir Hill.

Remarkably, those who responded had different stories about what they remembered seeing, but their overall recall coincided with my prevailing memory. Remember, this took place at least 65 years earlier than this writing. At first, I discounted some of their recollections and took a superior approach to what they said could not have happened the way they told them because my memory was better. After all, I was the one writing about a lingering memory I had carried around for years. It was an obsession!

After viewing the dead lady, my most vivid memory of the situation was the hexagonal shape of the coffin. So, I started trying to discover how and where the coffin was made. This approach allowed me to be objective. When I began contacting people and listening to their experiences, it opened up new investigative avenues.

For example, one friend said he remembered the stainless-steel coffin and seeing the sun reflect off it. My first reaction was to reject his memory because I knew stainless steel was not completely perfected and used until 1913. I have discovered, though, that there were many other forms and examples of stainless steel before 1913. I also had already determined that the coffin was not made before 1848, so how could it be that he saw stainless steel?

It was an epiphany for me, and I realized I must be open-minded and not discount anyone or anything. After all, as I said, this was some 65 years ago. We all see things differently, and with our young minds being traumatized at the sight of a dead body, my friend must have seen stainless steel. Or, perhaps the sun was reflecting off the glass face plate!

Another childhood friend, Kathy, says she removed a metal part attached to the coffin and took it home to her father. My first reaction was that the girls had not ventured upon Reservoir Hill during those days because I had never seen one up there. She said her father buried it in the backyard because he thought it was creepy. Gathering my thoughts, I found more pictures online of these types of coffins. Some had handles. Most had hinges or small metal pieces attached every few inches, apparently acting as welded seals. The metal part Kathy described fits the description of a weld from a coffin lid. I got all worked up and decided to get a metal detector, go down to Helena, and search in Kathy's backyard. This idea quickly passed as she told me the house had been sold years ago to make room for a business. She also said the lot had been paved over. I became determined to leave no stone unturned.

On *Facebook*, Joyce-Young-White recalled seeing the body adorned in Indian jewelry. She said she had a ringside seat, and because of the color of the remains, Jordan Funeral Home was dispatched to remove the coffin. Initially, I discounted this information. However, after opening my mind and doing more analysis, I concluded that the body probably turned to a darker color because of decomposition once the glass face plate was broken. Due to the racial climate at that time, it makes sense that the Negro funeral home was called into play. The body would not have been allowed to be reburied in the all-White Maple Hill Cemetery.

I can also understand why people felt the dead lady was an Indian Princess because her clothing appeared to be buckskin, just like I remember. Maybe it was, but it could have been just a frilly dress that turned brown due to decomposition. I was focused on the body and didn't remember any jewelry, but it's easy to understand connecting jewelry and buckskin to imagine it was an Indian Princess. It also makes sense that she could have been adorned in jewelry as her family wanted her nicely dressed, as she could be seen through the glass face plate of the coffin. People see different things, but all the distant memories make perfect sense. We all saw the same person.

Another person said the area west of the water tower had previously been an Indian burial ground, and there were rumors of discovering an Indian princess wearing white. It could have been an Indian burial ground in years past, but I doubt Indians buried their dead in iron coffins. The coffin we saw as children was unearthed east of the water tower, near the edge of the cliff overlooking the city of Helena. It doesn't mean Indian remains were not found on Reservoir Hill, but it's implausible they were found dressed so beautifully, wearing white gowns. I remembered talk of Indian burial grounds around the Helena Crossing area and knew some people had recovered several artifacts from there.

These rumors led me to look into the history of Native Americans. One particular discovery from the U. S. Indian Boarding School History stood out. Through the past two centuries, the United States and Canada enacted policies and passed laws requiring Native American children to attend boarding schools. The schools resulted from the United States' growth as they continued to advance westward and push the Native Americans off their lands. The government broke treaties it had previously signed and offered new land concessions in return for educating people on the reservations to where they had been pushed.

Children were removed from their families and placed in these schools. The idea was to change the culture and "civilize" or "Americanize" them. The Indian Removal Act of 1830 validated this, which basically was cultural genocide by reprogramming. Several Christian churches provided the schools, which the government funded as a way to integrate the Native Americans into the American culture. Over the years, hundreds of thousands of children were taken by force and compelled to learn and practice the ways of the White man. They were punished for speaking their native language or practicing traditional customs such as wearing traditional clothing or having long hair.

Many children were beaten, starved to extinction, or tortured if they disobeyed school rules. History has revealed that children died due to severe discipline and were buried in unmarked graves. Their classmates were forced to dig their graves. Many never saw their family again and were forced into manual labor. They were sent far away from their homes and scattered among 408 federal schools in 37 states in the U.S. They were also required to change their names. Unmarked burial sites are listed in 53 schools.

Canada practiced similar policies as late as the 1980s by trying to assimilate the Indian children, stealing them from their homes, and integrating them into The Native Children and Child Welfare System. The idea was to separate the children from their heritage. Many were adopted and raised without knowing anything about their ancestors. Others were left in the system, bounced to different foster homes, and never adopted.

The Catholic Church ran many boarding schools nationwide until 1969 when survivors revealed they suffered sexual, physical, and mental abuse for years. The Canadian government shut down its' last such school in 1997.

In 2006 and 2007, lawsuits called for the Canadian government to pay $4.7 billion and the Protestant Church to pay $9.2 million to all former students. The Catholic Church was ordered to pay $29 million but, by 2013, had only paid $1.2 million. In an appeal, the government sided with the Catholic church and dismissed the remaining amount, stating it had problems with fundraising. In 2021, Pope Francis publicly apologized for the atrocities, but no further payments were ever made. There have been 1,300 anomalies of potential unmarked grave sites found in Canada on the grounds of previous boarding schools.

Because of my earliest memory of seeing the body dressed in buckskin clothing, I deemed it necessary to check the possibility of it being a Native American. I have ruled out the case because Arkansas was not one of the 37 states where a boarding school was present. No other facts have fallen into place that would deem this scenario to have anything to do with an Indian Princess.

I was not the only kid who remembers seeing the lady clothed in buckskin. Stories, movies, tales, and other sources traditionally depict Indians (Native Americans) wearing buckskin. It's their culture! So, I can understand why rumors followed, characterizing the lady as an Indian Princess.

The facts are that Native Americans did not bury their dead in cast-iron coffins, particularly on Reservoir Hill. Each tribe performed a different variety of rituals, but none of them involved a cast-iron coffin. Most usually wrapped their deceased in their finest tribal clothing and buried them in various places.

For example, some were buried in hewn wood or sarcophagi made from whalebone. These two containers were as close as they got to an iron box. Other tribes placed the body on a cliffside and covered it with rocks. Some tribes killed a horse and buried it with the body.

The early Cherokees created high mounds of dirt to cover the body. Some tribes wrapped their dead in blankets and positioned them sitting up. The corpse was placed in an open hole, which was covered with canes to support layers of dirt.

The Sioux wrapped the body in fine clothing and laid it on a platform. The platform was then elevated into a tree and remained above the ground for a year before being taken down and buried.

After much searching and digging, I found a lady named Maria. Her heritage was not Native American. To my surprise, I suspect she never walked upon the soil of Helena, Arkansas, or even drew a single breath of air in Helena. If she did, it was only a brief time to visit her husband's grave and plan her final resting place next to him.

Maria's birth name was Maria Mariah Horstman. Her father was Anthony Horstman, and her mother was Catherine, with no maiden name available. Maria was born in 1807 near Brownsville, Pennsylvania, roughly 20 miles south of the Pittsburgh city limits. Other records claim her to be born in 1810. Because all documents in that era were handwritten, it took time to be precise when verifying information. Even more challenging is, in some cases, more evidence is needed.

Maria married Samuel James Clark. They made their home in Madison, Indiana, some 25 miles northeast of Louisville, Kentucky, on the shore of the Ohio River. Sam and Maria met in Pittsburgh because Sam worked on the Ohio and Mississippi Rivers. Looking back to chapter 10, Samuel James Clark was the Captain of the *General Brown* Steamboat, which exploded while docked in the Helena Harbor on the Mississippi River on November 25, 1838.

Another related article stated that *General Brown* was one of the fastest steamboats on the river. I surmise Sam and Maria were indeed deeply in love as Sam was always in a hurry to complete his long river journeys and return home as quickly as possible to be with Maria and his family.

Records for Samuel Clark state he was born in 1800 near Baltimore, Maryland. Other publications maintain that he was born in 1809. His remains were buried on Graveyard Hill, and I presume his body was so severely mangled that the decision was made to inter him there. Because embalming was not available until 1861, it would have been a long trip to have his remains returned home for burial, even if there were no injuries.

Sam and Maria had four children. Elizabeth was born in 1829, Maria in 1833, Anthony in 1836, and Catherine in 1839. So far, these dates are consistent. Catherine was born in April after her father died in November of the previous year. Census records have Maria's mother living with her and her children in the 1850s. It must have been difficult for Maria to raise her family without Sam being around.

I didn't uncover any account of Maria ever remarrying. She died in 1861, according to notes written by her fourth-generation grandson, Samuel James Clark, 1938-2017. Her body was shipped to Helena, Arkansas, to be buried near her husband, Captain Samuel James Clark 1st. Her age of 51-52 would have aligned with my childhood memory of the sight of her body and coincided with descriptions of people I know who saw her. She did not appear very elderly, and her body was intact. Simple common sense tells me that she had to have been embalmed because her body was not severely decayed or skeletal. The coffin looked ancient and fit the description of the ones made by Almond Fisk after 1848.

Also, in his notes, he says his father, Selby Anthony Clark, 1907-2010, and his wife, Lotha, visited Helena in 1976. They were trying to locate the grave sites of his grandparents Captain Samuel James Clark and his wife Maria. Selby Clark continued to write that he had the receipt for Maria's coffin and shipping box from 1861. They were unsuccessful for several reasons. First, the Battle of Helena in 1863 was attributed to the grave markers' loss and destruction, and in 1870, all known graves were moved to Maple Hill Cemetery. Also, years of soil erosion added to the disappearance of any overlooked remains. This information was recorded in the *Phillips County Historical Society Quarterly,* where my search for Maria began.

I graduated from high school in Helena in 1961. By 1976, when Selby Anthony Clark visited Helena in search of his great-great-grandparents, I had already finished college, completed a tour in Vietnam, and lived in Memphis, with my childhood memories of Helena in the rearview mirror.

Selby Anthony Clark lived in Bement, Illinois. He was an avid genealogist and kept detailed narratives and information related to his family history. He had written a letter to the Phillips County Library a couple of years before his visit, seeking to secure data on the location of the grave sites. Those still living in Helena in 1976 had no knowledge of the lady's body we saw in the 1950s. My research revealed that any reports were difficult to locate. So, Selby had to return to Illinois without the information he sought to complete his family genealogical records.

The death and burial of Maria also align with the information that she was buried on Graveyard Hill before the Battle of Helena in 1863. It also makes sense that because she was not a local, even if parts of her grave marker were found, no relatives lived in Helena and could not have come forward to have her moved to the new Maple Hill Cemetery when this was done in 1870.

Embalming was in its' infancy in 1861. Embalmers were still learning the new art of how much and how many different chemical solutions were necessary to perfect their jobs. No one knew for sure how long a body would remain preserved as this varied depending on the material makeup of the coffin. The Fisk coffins were airtight. Fisk purposely made them small to eliminate as much air as possible from being trapped inside. So, the weight and size of the body, along with the temperatures and humidity, also made a difference in the preservation process. The natural corrosive chemicals contained in the soil were an additional factor.

Part of my conclusion about the body being embalmed is based on what I learned from discussions with my friend Fay Van Valkenburg, who claims he broke the glass face plate of the coffin. Fay lived at the bottom of the hill. He told me that when he came upon the coffin, he sent his younger female cousin, who was with him, back to his house to retrieve a hammer. He said, "I thought it was a torpedo." Young minds will play tricks!

He recalls the deceased lady wearing a pink frilly dress and a blue bonnet. I remembered she was wearing buckskins, but I don't remember any bright-colored clothing. I estimate I saw the body within a few hours after he broke the glass or maybe the next day. Below is what he posted on *Facebook*.

> I lived below Reservoir Hill & saw the end of casket sticking out side of hill. I got my cousins Billy Hansen & Francis Rice to go up & find the casket, Billy & I dug the casket up & did not know what it was. It had a small window in one end that had fogged over. I sent Francis or Billy down to my house to get a hammer. When I finally got the hammer, I broke the glass & we all looked into the casket. Inside was a pretty girl dressed in Blue with a Pink bonnet. Her face was absolutely perfect, but as the air got to her, she began to decompose & turn to dust ! We will never Forget our experience! We ran away like a ghost was chasing us & went down to my house & told my mother. She got in touch with

> Doctor Mc Carty, who checked us out. He thought she had passed away due to an outbreak of Yellow Fever around the Civil War & was somewhat concerned that, due to casket being hermetically sealed, the disease might still be present. I would guess that I was around 6, so this would have been around 1953. To pin things down, there should be some sort of record about the move of all of the other graves to another location. Erosion was exposing all on the graves up on the hill. Freaked all of out!! & I for one will never forget our experience! Would be great to get details on the Graveyard, where all were relocated to & how most had passed! Also, what was the Graveyard named & 1st started? One of my most interesting Memories!!

My exploration led me to speak with an experienced licensed pathologist. She indicated that body decomposition could have easily turned the corpse and the clothing into the color brown after exposure to air. Thus, a frilly pink dress could have easily looked like buckskin.

Further searches about the burial of women in the 1800s have led me to discover that it was expected to bury them in loosely fitted dresses adorned with crocheted trim, another reason to confuse buckskin with frills.

Some people assume embalming will preserve a body forever. Of course, this is not the case and probably not necessary today because remains can be shipped rapidly without fear of decomposition. Also, the art of embalming is now a fine science designed only to last long enough for a body to be viewed by family and loved ones before burial.

I referred to two other finds of where people died in Kentucky and Louisiana approximately during the same era as Maria. These bodies were also unearthed in the 1900s. Both instances contained similar details to our discovery of Maria.

Here, decomposition had not taken over the bodies or clothing, and the coffins were made of iron. In the early days of such procedures, the embalmers were likely experimenting with properly using the required embalming fluids.

I searched extensively for any recorded clues verifying what may have happened to the body many of us saw on Reservoir Hill when I was a youngster. I have often wondered if I would have written this book if I had met Selby Clark on his 1976 visit. With my memory and his expert searching skills, the mystery of the lost lady may have been solved then. What's clear is that there was a body found during this time, and it's also clear it was a female. We also agree that our parents and the authorities were concerned the body may contain diseases, even though her corpse was in a nearly unsullied condition. Everyone wanted it to be expeditiously removed and safely relocated.

It needs to be clarified who she was and what became of her. Some said she was buried at a different cemetery, and others felt she was moved further to the western part of Reservoir Hill. No one will ever be able to provide a one hundred percent accurate account of every aspect of the events from the 1950s through today. Considering the lady in the coffin's birth, with the dates I have verified, her story is extended to over two centuries.

I have explored and examined Keeshan Lambert's funeral home journals for the 1950s. I have contacted Jackson Highly Funeral Home, which purchased the Black-owned Jordan Funeral Home, and they say they have no retained register. So, if Maria was moved to a different cemetery in the 1950s, the information is not recoverable in any known archive.

The coffin contained a glass face plate, and the body was well preserved, evidence that the person in the coffin had been embalmed. Without embalming, her body would have been wholly disfigured after so many years in the ground.

Recapping: Modern embalming did not begin in the U.S. until 1861. The correct formula of formaldehyde and other combined chemicals was still being perfected. The art of this procedure was new to the funeral industry, and I doubt it was used in Helena so quickly, as Maria died on June 16, 1861. Also, the Fisk coffin she was buried in was most likely manufactured in Cincinnati because Almond Fisk sold his patent to The Crane and Breed Casket Company of Cincinnati in 1853. I pointed out earlier that these coffins were expensive.

At this time, only a few people in Helena could probably afford coffins costing three times the price of wooden ones. I don't think there would be a need to use a glass face plate if the coffin was for a local because iron coffins with solid iron lids were also available. Maria's home was in Madison, Indiana, just a short distance down the Ohio River from Cincinnati. Benedict & Carter Company owned the *General Brown* steamboat. It was located in Louisville and employed Captain Clark. The Clarks lived on plot number 178 on the west side of Broadway in Madison. The cities of Cincinnati and Louisville were near, both on the Ohio River, making that part of the country more industrialized than Helena. So, I assume this type of coffin was more accessible for families living in the region.

I have had to piece together information as I identify bits in solving this mystery. It is like building a case with circumstantial evidence and is the direction I have been compelled to proceed, aided by conclusions. For example, my younger friend says he "saw the coffin from the bottom of the hill and broke the glass" face plate. He would have been between six and ten years old at the time. The coffin had been pulled entirely out of the ground when I saw it. The iron coffin alone would have weighed at least 200 pounds without the body. There is no way he could have managed something so large and heavy.

Several people who answered my *Facebook* post named the Hargraves brothers who dug up the coffin. I grew up and went to school with them. They were strong enough to handle such a feat. Also, a friend told me a third person was their frequent companion and continually hung out with them. Their sister, Ann, posted on *Facebook* that they told her about it. I remember seeing it in the afternoon after the body was exposed to the elements. Also, by this time, word had spread around the neighborhoods, and many people had viewed it.

I have searched extensively for months to locate any recorded periodicals at funeral homes or newspapers. As kids, we played on Reservoir Hill for several years after this incident and found no indication that the body had been relocated further to the western section.

My friend, Larry Killett, posted on *Facebook,* "I was there when the coffin was discovered, helped dig it up." He goes on to say, "The coffin was on Reservoir Hill. The only person that I remember with me that day was Clarence Henson (Pug). There were others present but I do not remember who…, we went to the Hill before school (Helena Jr. High) and chipped dirt so we could run and jump off the cliff, hit the soft dirt that had been chipped off, and rolled down to the bottom. That is what I remember!"

In another post Larry says, "Pug Henson and I did not remove it from the ground. We chipped out the form of the casket. I do not know who actually removed it. I remember that it was the color of tin or zinc, and it had a small window at the head. We could see that inside was a small girl with a light-colored dress, white or yellow. We left it exposed and went to school. After school we returned to the casket and found that the 'window' had been broken and you could not tell that it had been a little girl in the casket. Later, it was said she died of scarlet or yellow fever and that the authorities moved the casket further up the Hill and reburied it."

On July 15, 2022, I received a tip that someone had spotted part of a coffin exposed on the northwestern section of Reservoir Hill. I wanted to check out all possibilities, hoping this would be the coffin that I remembered as a kid. I had aspirations of it being relocated to this area. The temperature was 95 degrees, but I drove two hours to Helena to view the coffin. The kudzu was up to my chest when I arrived, blocking all visibility. It was impossible to spot any signs of it. I knew I would have to return during the winter when the kudzu was dormant.

I watched the weather for several months, waiting for a dry day with a pleasant temperature. As it turned out, New Year's Day 2023 was the day. Because college bowl games were being televised that day, this was a reasonable time to approach the hill discretely. I traveled to Helena and began searching for the coffin in the area described to me. To my overwhelming joy, I located part of an iron coffin protruding from a cliff 30 to 40 feet above a gulley. The kudzu was dormant but densely intertwined together. I managed to hold on to it while getting toe holds to scoot myself down until I reached the site. Relying on my memory, which I had carried around for 65-plus years, I began to pull back the kudzu. I was looking for a hexagonal coffin with a broken glass face plate on top and a space where a welded metal seal had been removed. To my disappointment, this was only the lid of an old iron coffin. It was rectangular shaped, solid iron, and grooved around the top with no hole for a glass face plate. It was on the side of the cliff, above the deep gulley, and it was tilted down toward the gulley. It was apparent that the coffin and body had been washed down into the gulley, leaving the lid lodged into the side of the hill. I estimate this occurred many years ago, and the body and coffin were probably buried below in 30 to 50 feet of eroded soil.

This was no doubt not my lost coffin! Looking back on my searches, the information that Joyce-Young-White posted on *Facebook* about Jordan Funeral Home moving the coffin must be accurate. It also proves that some coffins were left behind, but I have found no records to verify any other finds of such incidents over the decades.

Newspaper articles in October 1899 proclaimed that several bodies had been exposed due to the changing landscape. City authorities proposed "that bones, bodies, and caskets" be gathered up and placed in an area provided by Maple Hill.

Previously, in April of that same year, Maple Hill sold 35.9 acres of its property on the west side to Magnolia Cemetery, to be used only for African Americans. In the 1950s, we had no idea that Reservoir Hill had previously even been a cemetery, albeit an all-White cemetery. I have only found out this through my research. So, it makes sense that the Black-owned Jordan Funeral Home would have been called to remove the remains of the lady with a darkened skin complexion. Magnolia Cemetery would be the logical conclusion for her reburial. Only a wire fence divides the two cemeteries, and they remain divided for either all Whites or only African Americans. I have to make a significant conclusion that Maria was reburied inside Magnolia Cemetery without a marker.

A story in the *Helena Phillips County Quarterly* reveals about the bartender Patric V. Dunn of Dublin, Ireland. He was also killed in the *General Brown* explosion. I would imagine he and any other victims of the steamboat explosion were all buried near Captain Clark in wooden coffins. The city of Helena probably paid for some of the expenses and handled the burials as expeditiously as possible. Wooden coffins were the norm then, especially when circumstances required prompt decisions. It would have been almost impossible to transport a corpse many miles back to a person's home without considerable decay.

Since Maria died before the Battle of Helena, it's logical that she was buried near her husband, Samuel James Clark, in 1861 because his grave was marked. It's impossible to be sure, though, how near him she was interred because of the other 55 people who lost their lives in the steamboat explosion 21 years earlier.

The *Quarterly* describes a letter written by John M. Clark, dated October 25, 1839, almost a year after the death of his brother, Captain Clark, to his widow Maria. He relates how his tombstone was being made and was concerned it would be appropriately packed to prevent damage while being shipped from Indiana to Helena. The *Quarterly* further describes locating the headstone of Patric Dunn washed down the side of Graveyard Hill but no record of Captain Clark's. When growing up, we found no evidence of any tombstones.

The hill was dirt, with no rocks or ground cover. Severe land shifts were caused by natural soil wash. The coffin we saw was left atop the hill in an open space, approximately 25 yards southeast of the description of where the bones and bodies were washed up in 1900. This area was a flat section above the cliffs' edge. From what I have learned, I conclude that Marias' heavy iron coffin was left untouched by erosion for many years because it was located away from the hill's edge, while the others were made of wood and buried near the edge. Today, we can only presume that the victims of the *General Brown* explosion were left buried under tons of eroded soil or were moved in 1900 to Maple Hill in an unmarked area.

Two years after Maria was buried on Graveyard Hill, the Battle of Helena occurred on July 4, 1863. The 43rd Indiana Infantry Regiment took part in some of this battle and most likely contributed to some of the destruction of the tombstones of Samuel and Maria Clark.

Lieutenant Colonel Pace also assisted in the Union victory while leading a dismounted detachment of the 1st Indiana Cavalry, taking many Confederate prisoners.

Anthony Clark, the son of Maria, was drafted into the Union Army on August 5, 1863, at the age of 25. I don't find records of him ever serving in Helena with the Indiana Infantry. If he had, I would presume he would have tried to locate his parent's grave sites. Military records noted he served in Company A, 9th Indiana Infantry, and retained his parents' homestead until 1865 in Madison, Indiana. Anthony was an agriculturist (farmer). He moved to Bement, Piatt County, Illinois, in 1867 and married in 1872. His descendant, Selby Anthony Clark, continued to make Bement his home.

Sources:

Facebook, *Helena Friends*
Boardingschoolhealing.org
The National Native American Boarding School Healing Coalition
American Indian, Smithsonian Institution
en.m.wikipedia.org, American Indian boarding schools
Newspaper.com, *The York Gazette,* December 18, 1838
The *Helena Weekly World,* October 11, 1899
*Phillips County Historical Qua*rterly VOL 3 No 1, VOL 16 No 2
Ancestry.com, Civil War Draft Records Madison Township
Indiana 3rd district VOL 1
Bement, Illinois Funeral Home, March 9, 2010, Findagrave.com, Anthony Clark
blog.billiongraves.com, Native American Burial Rituals
National Museum of the American Indian magazine, Fall, 2022, Apologies are not enough by Barbara Bad Elk, pages 8-9, Summer, 2023, Homecomings, page 24

Chapter Fifteen

UNFALSIFIABLE

While writing this book, I had no idea I would finish with such a different outcome from how I wanted to tell my story. I tried to describe my boyhood experience of seeing my first dead person and then bring it all to a straightforward ending. It's been far from uncomplicated and effortless.

I'll be the first to admit I was a rookie searching for documentation. However, there is no difference when no recorded information exists because documentation was not required. For example, Indiana did not require birth or death certificates until 1882. Before this date, this type of material is only found with luck. It must be discovered through newspapers, family bibles, church directories, books, old letters, and other saved family history. Mostly, it requires knowing where to look and who to ask for specific data. Most families that have such information about their ancestors don't even know what they may possess.

Census entries are the only consistent reports. But, after reading, you must compare each ten-year lapse and then make an educated conclusion. Even then, there is little personal information about a subject.

Maria Moriah Horstman Clark and her husband, Captain Samuel James Clark, purchased their home in Madison, Indiana, in 1832 for $150. She lived in the house with her four children until she died in 1861. Piecing bits of information, I found she belonged to the First Baptist Church in Madison, Indiana, from 1847 through 1852.

Although I only have limited detailed information concerning the life of Maria, I have traced her lineage down to her fifth-generation granddaughter, Angie Clark Romine. I have spoken with her, and she has provided me with helpful information. I asked her to search for the receipt her grandfather, Selby Anthony Clark, reported he possessed for Maria's coffin and shipping box, but it was not found in the family notes. However, I found evidence from Vail's Funeral Home in Madison, Indiana, listing deaths for June of 1861. Maria is listed as passing away on June 16, 1861, just as Selby Anthony Clark had written.

This data is not precisely a receipt, but it lists the names of several people along with the cost of their coffins. Most of the coffins are listed at $2 to $3 each. The cost of Maria's coffin was $10. This clue indicates that her coffin was made of iron, as I pointed out in chapter two. Also of interest is the price of an additional box for $3, which was included by the funeral home. Only a few of the other people buried by Vail Funeral Home were charged for a box, and those without boxes were charged for a hearse. Maria's information does not list a charge for a hearse, which further proves the box was used for packing her coffin so it could be shipped to a different location for burial. Although the funeral home journal is not a receipt, it verifies Selby Clark's search that Maria was sent elsewhere for burial.

This entire venture has developed into a belief that I cannot disprove or prove beyond a shadow of a doubt. I liken it to the disappearance of Malaysia Airlines MH370 on March 8, 2014. With 227 passengers and 12 crew members, the plane vanished into thin air or the South China Sea. It was en route from Kuala Lumpur, Malaysia, to Beijing, China. No one knows for sure what happened to it. All people on board are presumed dead.

There are numerous similarities between flight MH370 and the information I have uncovered about the lady in the coffin. For example, I saw the body of an unidentified female in a coffin, and so did several other people. Flight MH370 was en route on its' prescribed flight path and was being monitored by air traffic controllers by radar when it lost communication after only 38 minutes into the flight.

No amount of searching has pinpointed the downed location of flight MH370, but multiple searches covering thousands of square miles have turned up only a few fragmented pieces of debris over nine years. The largest is the right flaperon with a confirmed serial number. No one knows what became of the coffin with the lady in it, and no one knows her identity, but witnesses saw it. Records of flight MH370 were recorded by radar, and all the documents are available. I have had to dig for all of my information.

I am confident I have unveiled the lady's identity in the coffin, but I cannot unconditionally guarantee it was Maria. I have no body, no coffin, no exact confirmed reburial site, no pictures, no DNA, or specific written account or dates to secure all of my searches. I have confidence that everything I have found makes perfect sense - Maria Moriah Horstman Clark was the lady I saw in the coffin in the last half of the 1950s. My memory of her face coincides with my perception of an average 50-year-old female. The adage "it looks like a duck, quacks like a duck," etc., certainly applies here as far as I am concerned, albeit circumstantial evidence and common sense. The most solid fact is that nothing disputes what I have concluded. It's frustrating when you know what you have is what it is and is unfalsifiable but can't locate that one last tangible fact. So many records have just disappeared as time has passed.

A big disappointment is that we cannot add a memorial similar to Petit Jean State Park as a site on Battery C. I hoped a story like this would draw tourists to Helena to see and hear the story of the lady in the coffin. People can still read about it here, draw conclusions, and even conduct their own research!

A bright personal upside of this search is that I have been on an unintentionally developed spiritual adventure. I could feel the presence of my ancestors, friends, and all the past residents of Helena and their families. A most delightful discovery was tracing Captain Samuel James Clark's family history and communicating with a member of his present-day family, Angie Clark Romine. Enjoying the vicarious rides I had on steamboats, was an additional delight.

Even if I didn't recover the coffin I had hoped to locate on New Year's Day of 2023, I did come away from Graveyard Hill/Reservoir Hill with a lasting memory and a surprising bonus, making it all worthwhile!

After inspecting the iron coffin lid and assessing my conclusions, I took my wife to the cliff's edge overlooking Helena. Growing up in New York, this was her first time on the hill. I had spent many hours during my childhood playing in this location. It was also near where I viewed the coffin as a kid. I expected the view from the top of the hill to be lower, as most memories like this appear more prominent when you are younger. It was entirely the opposite! The height of the hill towered over my memories.

When we finished sightseeing, we started to return to my truck parked at Battery C, approximately 300 yards away. Coming in our direction were an African-American gentleman and a young African-American lady. We introduced ourselves to Bill W. and his great-granddaughter. He had brought her to Helena from their home in Missouri to see the city where he grew up. He told me we had lived in Helena during the same era, only a few years apart, on the same street. He lived on the north end of College Street, and I was on the south. Coincidentally, the entrance to Magnolia Cemetery is on the north end of College Street. While talking, we discussed many of the same places, but our memories were distinctively different. I soon realized this was because we went to segregated schools. The Black kids and the White kids did not hang out together. We only saw each other from a distance, basically living in two different worlds in the same place. In the 1950s, I only gave a little thought. Now, as an adult, this thought saddens me.

He told me the highlight of his young life occurred in 1965 when the Voting Rights Act was passed. It made an enormous difference for him because he was allowed to transfer to Central High, the White public school, which propelled him to make a career in the Navy.

President Lyndon Johnson signed the Voting Rights Act of 1965 into law. It lifted tremendous burdens and obstacles for African American citizens when voting. Some of those restrictions included literacy tests, poll taxes, and many other serious barriers, such as harassment, intimidation, economic reprisals, and physical violence. It provided the right to vote for all, regardless of race or color.

While we were talking, one place we both found familiar was The Hollywood, located across the river on Highway 61 in Mississippi. If you have ever listened to the song *Walking in Memphis* by Marc Cohn, it can be very spiritual. Bill told me his grandmother, Muriel, was the person who played the piano at The Hollywood in the song. As the four of us turned to leave, I could see Bill and his great-granddaughter had driven to the top of the hill from the backside road in a very sporty Mercedes. I had never used that road in all my years while living in Helena. He offered to transport us back to my truck so we did not have to walk around through the tangled kudzu and low-hanging tree branches. It was almost mystical traveling down it as we rode back to Battery C. I felt comforted and at peace knowing we could now live together. Maria is at peace now, too!

These feelings led me to see our connection through our Creator. Here are the lyrics for *Walking in Memphis*. Google it and listen.

Put on my blue suede shoes
And I boarded the plane
Touched down in the land of the Delta Blues
In the middle of the pouring rain
W.C. Handy
Won't you look down over me?
Yeah, I got a first-class ticket
But I'm as blue as a boy can be

When I'm walking in Memphis
Was walking with my feet, ten feet off of Beale
Walking in Memphis
But do I really feel the way I feel?

Saw the ghost of Elvis
On Union Avenue
Followed him up to the gates of Graceland
Then I watched him walk right through

Now security they did not see him
They just hovered 'round his tomb
But there's a pretty little thing, waiting for the king
Down in the Jungle Room

When I was walking in Memphis
I was walking with my feet, ten feet off of Beale
Walking in Memphis
But do I really feel the way I feel?

They've got catfish on the table
They've got gospel in the air
And Reverend Green, be glad to see you
When you haven't got a prayer
Boy, you got a prayer in Memphis

Now Muriel, plays piano
Every Friday at the Hollywood
And they brought me down to see her
And they asked me if I would
To do a little number
And I sang with all my might
She said, "Tell me, are you a Christian child?"
And I said, "Ma'am, I am tonight"

Walking in Memphis (Walking in Memphis)
I was walking with my feet, ten feet off of Beale
Walking in Memphis (Walking in Memphis)
But do I really feel the way I feel
Walking in Memphis (Walking in Memphis)
I was walking with my feet, ten feet off of Beale
Walking in Memphis (Walking in Memphis)
But do I really feel the way I feel?

Put on my blue suede shoes
And I boarded the plane
Touched down in the land of the Delta Blues
In the middle of the pouring rain
Touched down in the land of the Delta Blues
In the middle of the pouring rain

Meeting Bill confirmed many thoughts about my journey in searching for the lady's identity in the coffin. I knew then that my childhood experience had a purpose and contained a story that must be told and a mystery that had to be solved. In addition, I realized this revelation was about how all people should live together for the common good. As Marc Cohn said, "*Walking in Memphis* is about a kind of spiritual awakening, one of those trips where you're different when you leave."

Maria never stopped loving her husband, Captain Samuel James Clark, because she must have arranged to be buried near him many years after his horrific accident. It had to have been a monumental task in 1861, considering where she lived and where he was buried.

Sources:

Walking in Memphis, Marc Cohn (Google)
National Archives.gov, milestone documents
www.pixsy.com
www.nfi.edu
www.hrc.utexas.edu
The Rev. Michael McCain, St. Mark's Episcopal Chruch
Walking in Memphis- Wikipedia

Chapter Sixteen

FOOLPROOF

While recalling, searching, reading, digging, assuming, concluding, and speaking with others, I wanted indisputable "foolproof" evidence of the lady's identity in the coffin. To a great degree, I have that! But, I may have only proven myself to be a fool. I take full responsibility for the endeavor that resulted in these conclusions.

I uncovered a flaw in my thinking about the *Helena World* ("*HW*.") Because the *HW* was the only local news source, I assumed all local events and newsworthy stories were reported in the paper.

It wasn't until a year into my search that I realized the microfilmed *HW* could not possibly be the complete source that reported kids unearthing a coffin containing a body on Reservoir Hill in the 1950s. I say this because many told me all of the original paper copies of it no longer existed and could only be found on microfilm in the Arkansas State Archives. No one at the Archives or in any of the libraries I contacted knew the original copies of the paper were tucked away in colossal binder-size files in the Tri-County Genealogical Society in Marvell, Arkansas, approximately 20 miles from Helena.

I received this tip from my lifelong friend Crystal Eastman, who still resides in Helena. I immediately made arrangements to view the original paper and acquired access to the files from my friend Patty Smith in Helena, a member of the Society. It took only a short time to look through three years of the original copies. It was much easier to review than the microfilm pages because there were no obstacles. I determined that the *HW* was different from the influential big-city papers with unlimited resources of reporters and staff writers. The *Helena World* was a small-town newspaper and did what it had to do to stay in business and remain profitable.

The *HW* had a formatted layout that followed each day. The front page's upper right-hand section consisted of a top state or national story from other well-known new sources like the *Associated Press*. The different parts of the front page consisted of a daily meteorological report, police reports, municipal court reports, and other national or area news acquired from other sources. It was expected to see a story about a local fender bender followed by the name of the owner's insurance company. Small house fires were prominently listed, followed by insurance company names.

It was amusing that reports of stolen automobile hub caps appeared almost daily. I'm sure this information was readily available from police reports and released daily to the *HW*. The insurance company's name was included in many little two-line descriptions of incidents. It may have been a clever way to report news and get free advertisements.

There were several sections containing half or full-page picture advertisements. I worked at C.E. Mayer Department Store during all four years of high school. Every morning before school, I would go to the store, sweep the sidewalk in front, and then deliver the daily ad to the *HW* office. Later that day, it was published in the paper.

Mr. Hurbert Harris worked for Mr. Mayer. Each day, he opened the store and put together the ad while I was sweeping

the sidewalk. I remember the manufacturing companies supplied the store with unique cardboard cutouts (similar to metal printing plates). Hubert would place a sheet of paper over the cutout and trace the image, holding a sideways lead pencil that exposed a large section of the lead. This procedure produced a picture of the goods to be sold. He wrote the price and pertinent information at the bottom of the manually created ad. This daily ritual went on for years and proved very effective in keeping the customers abreast of any new items being sold at C.E. Mayers Store. Mr. Mayer probably had a contract with the *HW* for daily ads, but the staple for the *HW* was the rows and rows of two- and three-line personal advertisements, which probably sold for $1 to $3 each.

Local stories were found on various areas of the front page and the second and third pages. However, none of these stories listed the author or reporter. As I saw some of these stories, I remembered them and recalled the incidents when they occurred. It became apparent they were written by Helena and Phillips County citizens and given to the *HW* to publish. Most notable were sporting events involving the local schools, weddings, and obituaries. Occasionally, there would be some pictures of the local beauties or debutants, but a family member or a friend usually wrote the story.

It was apparent that most of the information was acquired from other sources and posted in the *HW*. I'm sure the *HW* subscribed to a national news agency for the information it selected and included in each daily edition. As I mentioned, the *HW* did what it had to do to stay in business and be profitable. I think subscribers were satisfied with what they read.

With this revelation, I determined it would never reveal any information about us kids unearthing an old iron coffin on our playground. It simply did not exist because no one told the *HW* or wrote up the incident to have it published. The *HW* had no beat reporter to send and interview the parents or the kids. Everyone was occupied with protecting us from diseases. Apparently, someone had already called Jordan Funeral Home to have it removed. Maybe the police?

To shore up my proof and dispel some of my foolishness, I traveled to Madison, Indiana, in June of 2023 to look at where Maria Clark spent most of her life. Helena, unlike Madison, is a Delta city protected by a 60-foot levee. The levee was constructed over several years after the great flood of 1927. Madison is positioned on the banks of the Ohio River. There is no need for a levee because the Ohio River is in a valley. Helena is nearly the same sea level as the Mississippi River because it is located in the Delta, making a levee a necessary component for survival.

The Ohio River, however, did flood a small section of Madison in 1937, with the high-water mark reaching the southwest corner of Broadway and First Streets. Maria and Capitan Samuel Clark lived on Second Street, plats #177 and #178, just the next block north of First Street and a few blocks west. Today, those plots are street addresses 716-718. It must have been difficult for Maria to continue living so close to the river and to relive her tragedy each time she saw a steamboat.

Sam + Maria's house in Madison, Indiana located west of Broadway and known and designated on the plat there of by the number one hundred and seventy eight (#178). They paid $150 in 1832. Selby and Lotha went to Madison in the early 1970's to find information on Sam and Maria and located the house which was close to the Ohio river.

This is a picture of the house the Clarks called home beginning in 1832. Maria lived there until she died in 1861, and her son, Anthony, kept it for a couple of years after the Civil War and later moved to Bement, Illinois. I tried to find out what year this picture was taken, but it was unavailable.

I took this most recent photo of the houses at addresses 716 and 718.

Captain Clark worked for the Benedict and Carter Company, which owned the *General Brown* steamboat. His route generally started in Cincinnati, some 40 miles upriver from Madison. Benedict and Carter's office was located in Louisville, approximately 40 miles downstream. It would have been easy for Captain Clark to get to work. He could see the Ohio River from his front door and hitch a ride on one of the many passing steamboats up to Cincinnati or down to Louisville in just a few minutes. From there, he could begin his route aboard *General Brown*.

Maria and Samuel's house was only a few hundred yards from the landing. I can see why they chose to live in Madison; it is gorgeous, picturesque, and a small, visually charming city.

The downtown area consists of many shops, stores, and restaurants, while the residential neighborhoods consist of a mixture of restored old houses and new ones built to fit into their former surroundings.

My wife and I stayed at the Chandler Hotel in Madison. In the 1800s, it served as a livery stable. Now, it has been restored into a beautiful boutique hotel loaded with Madison's charm. The city continues to convert other old buildings into modern real estate while retaining the history and nostalgia.

Madison is unique because it has the country's most extensive contiguous National Historic Landmark District, consisting of over 1,500 buildings covering 133 blocks. Most are listed on the National Register of Historic Places.

While we were there, the *American Countess* riverboat cruiser was docked just a few blocks from Clark's home on the Ohio River. It, too, is a paddle-wheeler similar in appearance to the *General Brown*. We got to mingle with some of the passengers while touring one of the old mansions.

In the 1800s, when Captain Clark commandeered *General Brown*, hundreds of paddlewheel steamboats traveled along the many waterways in the United States. They served multiple purposes, from freighters to passenger carriers. Today, there are few cruise boats afloat on American rivers. Only a few use paddlewheels and none are steam-powered. The paddlewheels are added and designed for nostalgia to retain the past representation of the steamboat. However, today's boats consist of the latest technology and luxurious accommodations but do not transport commercial goods as did the packets on the day of the steamboat.

In addition to getting a firsthand look at the area of Madison where Samuel and Maria lived, I wanted to check out the church Maria attended from 1847 to 1852. The First Baptist Church of Madison is located on Vine Street, only a few blocks from her house on Second Street. She lived there as a widow with her mother and four children until she died in 1861. The proximity of the beautiful Chandler Hotel was an added plus for our visit because all my points of interest were within walking distance.

In my inquiry, I found that the church continues to operate as the oldest Baptist Church in Indiana's history. It was established in 1807, just a few years before Maria was born. I initiated communication with Kelly at the church. She confirmed Maria was a member in the 1800s and sent me a picture of the congregation found in Maria's file. I hoped to establish that Maria was one of the members pictured.

Kelly was very generous in helping me and arranged for me to meet Paulina Giltner. Paulina is a long-time member of the Church and wrote *A Short History of First Baptist Church* in 1977. When I met Paulina, she was 105 years old. She didn't look a day over 80, was very sharp, and retained a wealth of historical information.

The picture of the church congregation, found in Maria's file, indeed was taken in the church. That room is still in use today. The photo was exceptionally clear to have been taken in the 1840s. One of my questions for her was to establish a possible timeline of when the picture was taken. I focused on the light sconces in the wall behind the posed people, hoping to determine if they were fueled by gas. If they had been gas-powered, this would have confirmed that the picture had been taken before 1852 when Maria was still a member.

However, electric lighting was not widely established indoors in this country until around 1925. Paulina said the lighting in this picture could have been fueled by gas but was most likely converted to electricity later. I still hoped this was an excellent opportunity to expect that one of the ladies in the picture was Maria. However, all of my speculative hopes came crashing down when it was pointed out to me that the legs of the women in the photo were uncovered. Such displays of female flesh during this era would have been extremely uncommon. Still, I was hopeful to make a connection to Maria being in the picture. I didn't think that much flesh was exposed! But, these questionable doubts concerning the clarity of the image helped me realize it had to be taken much later than 1852 after Maria had already left the church.

In addition to my hopeful speculation about the lighting, Paulina reported in her book that the church in 1847 was a small "frontier church" located initially on the existing property, just behind the present-day church. She said perhaps the lighting was changed from candles to kerosene lamps, squelching my hopes of Maria appearing in the membership picture.

Transcripts show Maria transferring her membership from Wirt Baptist Church in 1847 to the First Baptist Church. Wirt Baptist was over seven miles away from her home, compared to the First Baptist, which was only a few short blocks away. She could have virtually walked in 10 minutes or less.

In 1847, the First Baptist membership was at 150 and growing. Because of the growth, the church committee decided to build a larger building by "raising $10,000 by subscription to cover the cost of construction." The committee even considered merging with the Church of Disciples, commonly called Reformers, to solve their need for the necessary finances. Instead, they proceeded to use the power and confidence of the committee by taking steps to install "strict discipline."

My observation is that the "subscription" became mandatory. It may also be coincidental that Maria felt uncomfortable or could not afford to uphold her subscription, so she left in 1852. I have not uncovered any records of her transferring to another church. First Baptist records reveal she was "dismissed." This term means she ended her membership.

In 1853, construction began to erect the new church building. 1854, the first prayer meeting and worship service occurred in the basement. In September of 1860, the sanctuary was finished and used for divine worship. Someone had written, "The decade of the 1850s was bleak and spiritually depressed." So much effort had been spent on erecting a new building and raising money that the church itself suffered. They also said, "We as a church are in peace and fellowship with each other but lukewarm in religion. We are very much impoverished."

While there, I visited the site of the present-day First Baptist Church of Madison. It stands with a solemn presence. I was surprised that it is well over 160 years old and still looks new and beautiful. Today, it has a thriving membership and recently produced Vacation Bible School for 250 children with 150 volunteers participating. Its origins trace back to a crude log cabin with 15 members in 1807.

I have not located any other information related to the rest of Maria's life. Much of the history of our lives is made up of known facts, records, and hand-me-downs. Considering what was available from past years, I have uncovered much about Maria's life. Although others remember this story differently, it makes my account more accurate. I will always have a visual image of Maria lying in the coffin dressed in a buckskin jacket, clothing worn by people living on the "frontier." I regret that she is not laid to rest forever beside her husband as she had intended.

Sources:

Streetside History, Flood of 1937, Madison, Indiana
Piatt County Historical and Genealogical Society, Bement, Illinois
A Short History of First Baptist Chruch, Madison, Indiana by
Paulina Giltner
Touring Madison, Indiana on foot Steve Petkoff 2023
First Baptist Church Madison, Indiana
Madison Area Chamber of Commerce

Milton Keynes UK
Ingram Content Group UK Ltd.
UKHW022106110624
443988UK00016B/832